LOCAL WALKS

SOUTH BEDFORDSHIRE AND NORTH CHILTERNS

Vaughan Basham

A comprehensive book of circular walks in this delightful rural area.

Walking in the countryside provides healthy exercise, but, with this book as his companion, the rambler will also be led to many interesting discoveries. An appropriate theme has been selected for every walk, and a stimulating introductory article sets the scene.

Full practical route information and comments are also provided, plus specially drawn maps.

The author, Vaughan Basham, has lived in and explored the area all his life. His keen interest in social history has led to a continuing involvement in heritage affairs, conservation projects, local organisations and charities.

Scouting and the Outward Bound schools were influential in his love of the countryside and, together with his wife Una, he has always been an enthusiastic rambler.

GU00691754

To Una

Second Edition Preface

The book has been remarkably well received, but after two reprints an updating of the bus routes and one or two walk amendments were needed for this new edition.

It was always intended that a walks book for North and Mid-Bedfordshire would be written – this is now a reality, appearing concurrently with this new edition and written in a similar format.

In the course of my wanderings many interesting and curious places were encountered and such observations will form the basis of an eventual new illustrated book on this fascinating county of Bedfordshire.

Vaughan Basham

First published July 1988
by The Book Castle
12 Church Street, Dunstable, Bedfordshire
Reprinted 1989 (twice)
Second Edition July 1990

© Vaughan Basham

Printed by Antony Rowe Ltd., Chippenham

ISBN 1 871199 75 1

Cover photograph taken from the foot of Ivinghoe Beacon at the Ivinghoe Aston turn, looking north-east.

© Vaughan Basham

Contents

Contents

Introduction

The north Chilterns afford some surprisingly good walking country. Most of the walks are of a simple nature, or can be shortened, as an encouragement for those just discovering the pleasures of walking in the countryside. Brief background articles appear throughout the book with the intention of increasing interest and observation.

The walks described in this book are leisurely and· straightforward employing where possible green lanes, bridleways and well used paths rather than roads. Landmarks are given as a guide plus some distances.

Another feature of the walks is the fact that they are all, with one exception, capable of being linked one with another with the assistance of Ordnance Survey maps. Also, alternative starting points can be chosen instead of the one recommended.

N.B.
a) Views expressed in the book are those of the author, who also takes responsibility for any errors that may have been overlooked.
b) Work carried out by farmers, youth projects or Manpower schemes may necessitate occasional variations from the basic routes described.
c) For their protection the author has deliberately omitted naming sites where rare species of flora may be found.
d) The author c/o The Book Castle would be grateful to be notified in writing of any changes or ambiguities encountered by walkers using this book, so that amendments might be incorporated in any future edition.

Vaughan Basham

Acknowledgements

I would like to thank my friend George Marshall for his companionship on many walks throughout the Chilterns and the Vale of Aylesbury.

Advice came from Beds C.C. Leisure Department and the County Ranger Service, who are caretakers of much of Bedfordshire's countryside, with responsibilities ranging from cleaning-up to large conservation and access schemes. David Henden helped with the Upper Lea Valley section notes.

Thanks are also due to the National Trust for their help and information.

The Luton & District Bus Co. provided considerable information on their services in the area. This is condensed into a table at the rear, as well as being incorporated in the walks' information.

Information on local butterflies has been checked by Greg Herbert of the Beds. and Northants. Branch of the British Butterfly Conservation Society.

Vaughan Basham

Maps and Map-reading

Rambling books seldom say anything about maps and mapreading – a considerable omission really. Browsing over maps, then relating them to the countryside, is an exciting occupation. For example, one looks at map symbols then recognises the features on the ground, or one notes the closeness of contour lines giving a measure of the steepness of slopes. The Ordnance Survey include books on elementary mapreading in their growing list of publications.

When walking, a sense of direction and position assumes a significant importance, and so a compass may become very necessary in big expanses of open countryside or even in large fields, especially when the mist comes down.

History

Ptolemy in Greece nearly 2000 years ago collated all geographic knowledge then drew maps, but it was not until circa 1250 that the monk Matthew Paris produced a map depicting Gt. Britain. Though inaccurate it set down pilgrim ways, and marked several hundred towns plus a number of rivers. From Tudor times mapmaking became more regularised, with leadership in the skill of accuracy, engraving and surveying shifting variously between France, Holland, Germany and Gt. Britain.

Several factors precipitated cartography. New owners of monastic lands after the Dissolution wanted a record, and the counties as a loose unit of administration created a demand for the entrepreneurial printers. The latter commissioned atlases from the new breed of men calling themselves surveyors, while speculative ventures, printing initially from copperplate, were followed later by steel engravings, as woodcuts had long been abandoned for this sort of work.

John Ogilby introduced strip maps in bookform for travellers on the main highways in the 17th century, and the Royal Society for Arts commenced awarding prizes for county surveying maps in the mid-18th century. This field of activity thereby gained its due recognition.

Another milestone came in 1675 when John Flamsteed, as first Astronomer Royal working in the Sir Christopher Wren Observatory in Greenwich, published star almanacs, which, coupled with the fine chronometers constructed by John Harrison, gave this country supremacy in navigation. This extended into world-wide mapping as epitomised by Capt. James Cook. Trade was the spur.

The inspiration for improved mapping was partly military. In 1746, at the battle of Culloden, inadequate roadmaps had proved a major military disadvantage. General Wade set about rectifying the surveys, then improved the roads and bridges in Scotland. The Royal Engineers and Royal Military Surveyors were responsible for nationwide surveying, aided by draughtsmen and engravers together with local surveyors.

National involvement in map-making came in 1791 with the founding of the Ordnance Survey, housed in the Tower of London. The private publishing of maps, each usually an improvement on its predecessor, has continued right up to the present.

Very early in the history of map-making the idea of triangulation was recognised for acurate surveying work. This is seen today as the familiar Trig. Points – hilltop reference places for mounting theodolites in three vee grooves on concrete blocks, secured to three rings to prevent the instrument from being blown away.

For two centuries the scale of 1" to the mile was employed, with reliefs shown hachured all black, printed with hand colouring on private maps. The introduction of contours, specific colour representations for roads etc. and the regularising of map symbols, coupled with the great accuracies achieved, made Britain the best mapmakers in the world. Britain teaches cartography in colleges, undertakes surveying commissions, especially in the developing countries, and founds surveying departments there.

Interestingly, the first edition of the one inch Ordnance Survey of England and Wales published in 1834 is now available as a series of reprints by David & Charles Ltd.

Map-reading

Mapreading is not such a mystery as some people imagine, for, given the inclination, all can grasp the essentials. To begin, take an area that you know like the back of your hand and compare it with the representation on a map. Then consider an area in the countryside you only marginally know, identifying features depicted on the map to build up a comprehensive picture in your mind, all in the comfort of your own armchair. Experienced mapreaders can predict what lies ahead purely by 'reading' the maps as they walk along.

The symbols appearing on the R.H.S. of all Ordnance Survey maps reveal all when interpreted – hills, gridlines, woods, even pubs. It is worth noting that the grid squares on the 1:50,000 Second Series of maps in pink covers (Landranger) represent 1 kilometre square. For a simple conversion remember 1 kilometre equals 5/8 (0.625) of a mile making the scale about 1¼" to the mile.

Out in the country the map can be 'layed' with the land by using a compass. Either find the north and line up the map, as north is always at the top of the map, (strictly a magnetic correction should be made but is not of major importance usually). Or the more usual method is to start by finding exactly where you are on the map, then aligning distinctive features in the countryside, such as churches, roads, gridlines etc. in several directions, so that they appear in true 'lines of sight' for the correct map orientation. Confidence grows with experience.

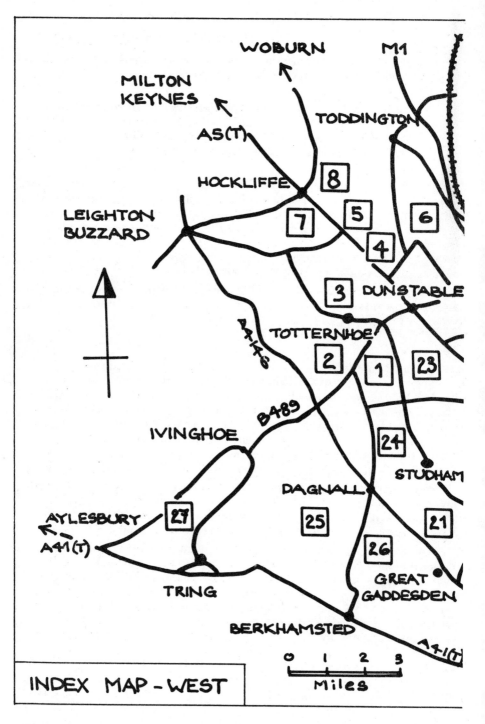

INDEX MAP - WEST

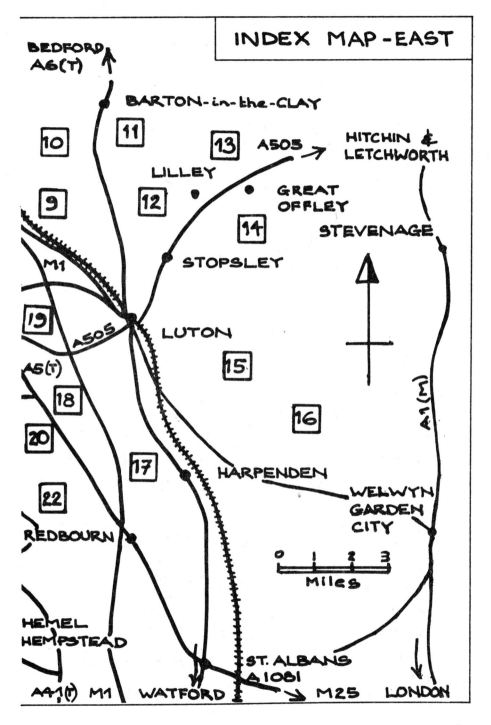

The Country Code

- Guard against all risk of fire
- Fasten all gates
- Keep dogs under proper control
- Keep to the paths across farm land
- Avoid damaging fences, hedges and walls
- Leave no litter – take it home
- Safeguard water supplies
- Protect wild life, wild plants and trees
- Go carefully on country roads on the R.H.S. facing oncoming traffic
- Respect the life of the countryside

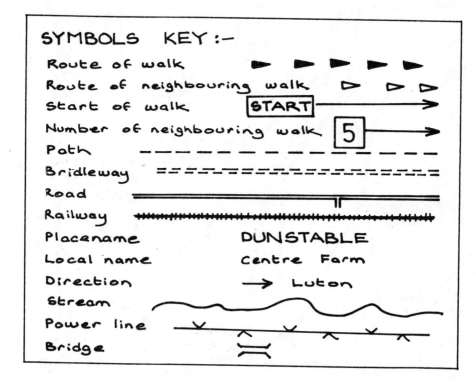

Butterflies of the Chalk Downlands

Places included: **DUNSTABLE DOWNS**

Length of walk: 4½ miles (or 2½ miles).

Grid Ref: Sheet 166 007214

Parking: Layby on the Whipsnade road or in Pipers Croft (2nd turning on left on Whipsnade Road).

Bus services: 43, 61, 69, 245 and 343.

Public Houses: The Pheasant (West Street, Dunstable).

Walk Links: A broad green trackway at the eastern end of the gliders' landing field, leads direct to Wellhead, the start of Walk 2 (met on the return leg of this walk). Also, the Information Centre on the top of the Downs is the starting point of Walk 24.

Notes 1: A shorter variant of this walk but in an anti-clockwise direction and of 2½ miles duration is described, commencing from the car park by the Information Centre. Grid Ref: 008198.

2: By crossing the road and walking a short way beside the golf course from the Information Centre excellent views over Dunstable are obtained, with the Warden Hills as the skyline in the east. St Albans cathedral can be seen in the south, and the skyline is north London.

BUTTERFLIES OF THE CHALK DOWNLANDS

Around 30 of Great Britain's 58 butterfly species can regularly be found amongst the north Chiltern Hills, the finest area in Bedfordshire for butterflies, but they do need grassland and special plants. Recently scrub has invaded their breeding and feeding grounds — hence the clearance policies. Their food plants range from brassicas (cabbage family), nettles and grasses right up to oak trees, whilst their complicated four stage life-cycle often takes 12 months for completion.

A few notes on the chalk downland butterflies might help stimulate an interest.

Small Blue, once known as the Bedfordshire Blue, is the smallest English butterfly with a wing span of 25mm, feeding on kidney vetch in the caterpillar stage from July onwards, eggs being laid in June. In the spring it takes on the

11

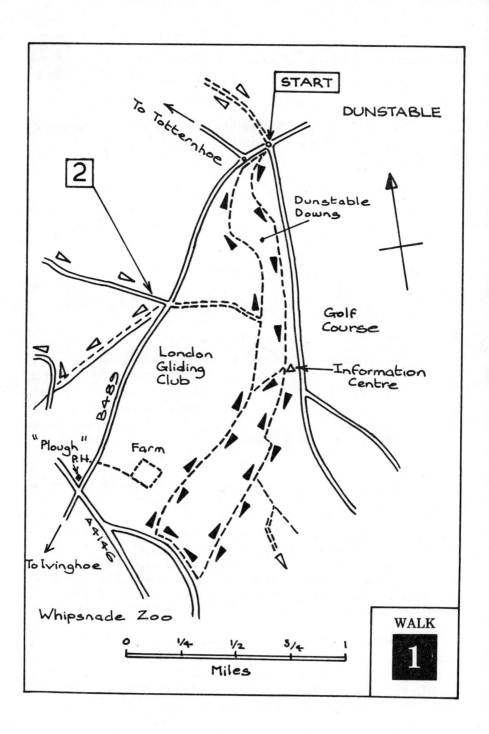

START

DUNSTABLE

To Totternhoe

2

Dunstable Downs

Golf Course

London Gliding Club

Information Centre

B489

"Plough" P.H.

Farm

A4146

To Ivinghoe

Whipsnade Zoo

0   1/4   1/2   3/4   1
Miles

WALK

1

chrysalis form, emerging as a butterfly from May. The Meadow Brown is the most common butterfly in the grasslands around Dunstable, so called from its dark brown coloured wings and requirement of meadow grasses as a caterpillar. Another distinctively marked butterfly, the Green Hairstreak, gets its name from the fine row of white dots on its green underwings. The Grizzled Skipper, whose markings are dotted white on brown, is a springtime butterfly, feeding in the caterpillar stage on wild strawberry plants. Other butterflies include Chalkhill and Common Blues, Large and Dingy Skippers, Brown Argus and Orange Tips, all species found in the wilder areas and especially Dunstable's chalk downland.

Caterpillar foodplants and their abundance is the key for butterfly populations, most of them specialist feeders. The seasons determine when they hatch as caterpillars for their nectar requirements. Grasses, trefoils, rockroses, vetches, dogwood and cuckooflower are amongst the flora used by our local butterflies along with the above-mentioned plants in their diets.

The Ringlet, although feeding on grasses, prefers damp grassy spots in hedgerows and wood margins, which is indicative of the variety of habitats that butterflies require, without mentioning those that have a preference for woodland, marsh and heathland with their indigenous flora.

Members of the British Butterfly Conservation Society not only record and monitor butterfly populations but also manage a number of sites for wildlife and butterflies in particular.

The Bedfordshire and Northamptonshire Branch of the BBCS has produced a booklet entitled 'The Butterflies of Dunstable Downs', a guide to the species found on many of the downland sites mentioned on these walks.

Sites of particular interest for butterflies in the area covered by this book include:

Ashridge .... National Trust
Barton Springs .... National Nature Reserve
Dunstable Downs .... Beds County Council & National Trust
Ivinghoe Beacon .... National Trust
Sewell Cutting .... Beds County Council
Sharpenhoe Clappers .... National Trust
Stockgrove Country Park .... Beds County Council
Sundon Hills .... Beds County Council
Totternhoe Knolls .... Beds County Council

WALK

DUNSTABLE DOWNS

Dunstable Downs offers an area of good walking particularly suitable for those who have come by car and want to explore rather than just sit in their cars. This walk offers more than just a short stroll along the top or the short descent from in front of the Information Centre to the London Gliding Club field. The steep scarp slopes provide up-currents for hang-gliders; gliders can also be seen riding in the thermals, gaining altitude.

The Downs is virtually a free roaming area, but two adaptable alternative walks are suggested.

Grand Circular (clockwise) distance 4½ miles.

Basic Circular (anti-clockwise) distance 2½ miles.

Grand Circular

The start of this walk is at the top of West Street, though the parking is not particularly easy, so use nearby roads if the layby is full. As an alternative the Information Centre can be the start.

Commence from the Whipsnade Road corner, ascending the mown grassy slopes up onto the skyline, with trees fringing the edges. The housing on the left stands on the site of the California open-air Swimming Pool, which once had a ballroom and Go-Kart track within its complex, and was previously an (exhausted) chalk quarry working. Into sight come the distinctive mounds of the Five Knolls which are barrow burial sites of the Early Bronze Age excavated at one time by Mortimer Wheeler. And now on to the natural bowl at this end of the Downs known as Pascombe Pit, traditionally the venue of Orange Rolling on Good Friday.

Sheep once grazed these downs and so there was no scrub. These open places saw military manoeuvres by the local militia in the Napoleonic Wars, hence the name of the West Street pub 'The Rifle Volunteer'. Army signalling, Home Guard and mortar practice took place up on these downs at various times. The little depressions found along the top were WWII motor firing positions, firing canisters containing small silk parachutes. Nowadays on Saturday afternoons in winter-time, television mobile relay stations are often found beyond the Information Centre relaying football coverage of league matches.

From Pascombe Pit we take a hilltop walk passing the Dunstable Downs Golf Club entrance, but it is the views on fine days that are the principal feature. Below lies the Vale of Aylesbury and beyond is Oxfordshire through to the Cotswolds. Although one can only see as far as Ivinghoe Beacon, the Chiltern Hills – and this is the northern extremity – continue southward as far as the River Thames at Goring Gap. The large scale of Dunstable Downs was created in the cretaceous period and shaped by ice and erosion – the 'dipslope' goes back into the London Basin.

Onwards then to the Information Centre which you really must visit. It is open from spring through to the autumn, and includes a snack bar and toilets. These flanks of the Downs have people working on them in the winter months clearing scrub, otherwise they would get overgrown and block out a number of views since they are no longer grazed. Cutting back helps the butterfly populations and all forms of wildlife.

Continue in the direction of Whipsnade on the main path past the emergency glider take-off grass slope and into a broad path through the dense scrub belt. On reaching the open fields follow the bridleway on the upper left-hand in the treeline. This is your guide right the way through to the Whipsnade Downs car park nestling out of site in a depression alongside the B4540 road on the way to the zoo. This is Bison Hill by association with the animals in the paddock across the road. Seek out the path that follows the perimeter fence above the road, but do not cross into the enclosure. The well-made path descends the hill bringing you out by the road, so be careful. Do not go out onto the road itself as it joins the foot of the Downs path.

The arching branches create the effect of a tunnel, which is regularly cleared throughout its length. We return beside farmland, not so far away from a large piggery unit. Initially National Trust ground is traversed, then in continuing one arrives at the broad spaces outside the gliding club's field. The much used path from the Information Centre is encountered in this vicinity but our walk makes no ascents. It utilises the wide grass stretches along the foot of the downs, making a turn in Pascombe Pit and, on a constant contour, rounds the spur of the range until funnelled onto the path at the ends of the Tring Road gardens. With the steep flank of the hill at your right hand elbow the path emerges at the familiar slope of the downs, a boon for winter sledging.

Basic Circular

This excursion starts from the Information Centre. We commence by walking down the slope in front of the Centre arriving at the glider takeoff field. Turn towards Whipsnade and it is found that a well used path is at the foot of the slopes. Without difficulty continue right through to the Whipsnade road, passing an extensive piggery.

Do not go out onto the road for, at your left hand side at the end, the well-made path rising beside a fenced-off field is discovered. Continue to the Whipsnade Downs car park and then use the path which brings you out onto the brow. The way ahead takes you out to Whipsnade Common but for this walk we turn left through the pedestrian gate beside the steel field-gate and from this meadow fine views of the Downs are gained. In fact this is the main reason for doing this particular walk as they are seen to great advantage and as we return alongside the right hand hedgerow their form becomes more pronounced. On reaching the scrub belt near the finish the bridleway through is easily seen midway down the end of the last field.

On passing through, the familiar area of open grasslands around the Centre is recognised and one can observe the distinctive outline of Ivinghoe Beacon in the west.

Of Mills

Places included: **TOTTERNHOE - EATON BRAY**

Length of walk: 5 miles (or 4½ miles).

Grid Ref: Sheet 165 999204

Parking: Roadside at Wellhead on minor road to Totternhoe, opposite the London Gliding Club entry in Tring Road.

Bus services: 43, 61, 69, 245 and 343.

Public Houses: Cross Keys, Farm Inn, The Bell, (all in Totternhoe).

Walk Links: Sections of Walks 3 and 4 meet on Castle Mound in Totternhoe.

OF MILLS

Without doubt one of the most endearing buildings of the countryside is the mill, be it of the wind or water variety. By their very nature windmills were prone to the ravages of storm, capricious winds, fire (airborne flour in a confined space being highly combustible) and neglect. Chronologically there are the postmills of the Tudor and earlier period, the multisided wooden smockmills and finally the 19th century brick tower pattern. The latter two both have caps that could turn the sails into the wind by a fantail, whereas with postmills the 'buck' or body moved. Common sails had cloths reefed onto framework, but later patent sails required no stopping and tying, as they had spring loaded shutters that could be sprung in stormy conditions. And yes, the windshafts were fitted with great bandbrakes for stopping rotation, but very slowly for fear of fire or disintegration. Oil, gas or steam engines stood by in the latter mills as wind is so unreliable.

So long as water could be stored in ponds, watermills were in a better position and they have had a history possibly even longer than their cousins. Whether using undershot, breastshot or overshot wheels dependent upon local conditions, by their very circumstances more watermills survive. As a means of power they were harnessed not only for cornmilling but for cattle feeds, paper-making, and gunpowder manufacture. They gave their name 'mills' to the great north country wool and cotton enterprises all driven by gigantic waterwheels.

Whether windpowered or waterpowered the gearing turned the 'wallower,'

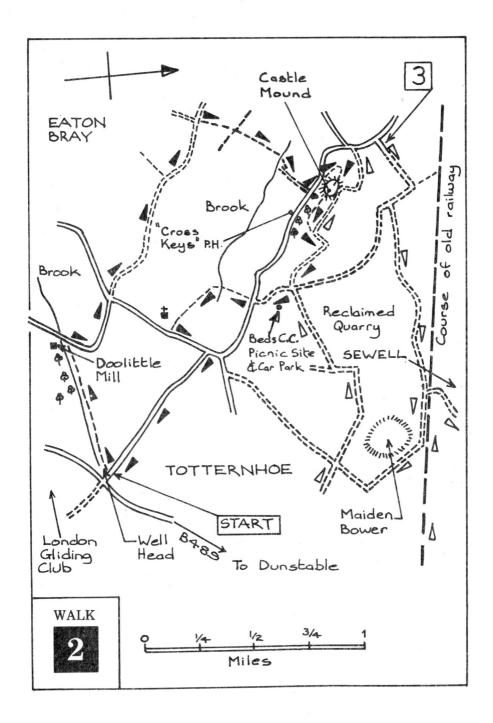

EATON BRAY

Castle Mound

3

Brook

"Cross Keys" P.H.

Brook

Reclaimed Quarry

Doolittle Mill

Beds C.C. Picnic Site & Car Park

SEWELL

Course of old railway

TOTTERNHOE

START

Maiden Bower

London Gliding Club

Well Head

B489

To Dunstable

WALK 2

0   ¼   ½   ¾   1

Miles

the bevel that drove the stones and all the other ancillaries, sackhoist, sifters and cornfeeders.

Possibly one of the most unusual mills in the country is the Doolittle Mill in Totternhoe, harnessing either water or wind. It is now crying out for restoration work and is recognised by Bedfordshire C.C. as a worthy case. An interesting observation is that the name Doolittle was often given to the first mill on a stream with its inadequate water supply, hence in this very special case seeking power from that extra element.

All water- and windmills are recorded on Ordnance Survey maps, and fortunately the Pitstone windmill and Ivinghoe watermill can be visited.

TOTTERNHOE, EATON BRAY

This is a most rewarding area for walking and is easy going, but the main features are the circle of hills and the streams with associated wildlife including dragonflies in season. Just as Anglesey provides an excellent vantage point to see the sweep of Snowdonia, so this walk enables you to take in the range of the Chilterns on Dunstable's doorstep.

Wellhead is a tributary of the River Ouzel, being a natural spring set in a hollow now surrounded by trees and in the care of the 1st Totternhoe Scouts, who have done a magnificent clearing-up operation in recent years. On the northern side of this notable spot is a bridleway which has a gated entrance and is the clearly-defined start of our perambulation. After a short while it descends to run alongside the tree canopied stream passing by the rear of a battery chicken rearing station, and at the footbridge can be seen how choked the stream is with weed. All in all, the setting is pleasant and the Doolittle Mill comes into sight on the far side of mature ash, sycamore and willow trees that surround the mill-pond. It is a composite mill which worked from water or wind, with the wheelhouse set between the two buildings, and the millhouse itself is of a 'double-pile' construction with a central chimney stack.

Turn right here utilising the road, and see the striking profiles of Ivinghoe Beacon and the silhouette of Edlesborough church on its mound. On passing the Warehill Equestrian Centre, with a covered riding area where they make a point of catering for the disabled rider, St Giles church set in the trees captures the near distance demanding attention; then move on to the tee road junction in front. Cross the road and enter the bridleway ahead, which can at times be quite muddy due to horse-riding, continuing across hedgeless fields to the outskirts of Eaton Bray. Follow the tall hedge in a northerly direction using a way that comes up from the left, and arrive at a main crossing of ways.

There is a farm here with a row of poplars nearby, and it was near here that Wallaces had their famous carnation nurseries, sending them out over considerable distances. By the black-boarded barn but on the other side is an asbestos barn on a brick footing which has an arrow post alongside showing the track used. It was on the green arrow route but you now turn right taking the yellow sign indicated. Further along is a crossing of paths and a stile appears. This is taken and the hedge followed at your right hand side up and over a bridge. Then make a diagonal crossing of this orchard to the side of Damson Cottage which has a flint rear walling but brick front facing — this part of the world was well-known for the damson trade used in dying hats in years gone by. You are now in Chapel Lane rising steeply to the Totternhoe Middle end.

An alternative return omitting Castle Hill is described at the end of this section.

Turn left at the road but if you are in need of a drink the 'Cross Keys' is nearby on your right hand side. Take the road passing a food and grocery shop, then soon after passing the White House on the first bend a signed footpath can be found entering the trees on the other side of the road. The first part is canopied in greenery crossing a stile, then after 100 yards or so an opening is encountered and rising irregular slopes make for the skyline, these being old quarry tips grassed over. Now a path can be found making for the summit. This is managed sitework by the Beds and Hunts Nature Trust which is allowing ash trees a certain amount of colonisation. Then on to the top which is through the bushes in front. You cannot get lost. You are now on the motte or mound of a nearly 1,000-year-old castle with its encircling ditch and the bailey or fortified open space on the southern side. But what a view, a full 360° taking in the zoo, Ashridge and the Beacon hills above Risborough, with Oxfordshire as the far skyline, then a big chunk of Bedfordshire through to the Warden Hills above Luton, and the Downs each side of Dunstable. Magnificent.

Here we are above the beech slopes and above the adjacent road, with a path encircling the whole area. It is worth coming back for the occasional stroll. Leave on the far side of the bailey-yard beyond the row of beeches out in the left hand corner, and continue forward joining a left hand bridleway on coming out of the bushes. This takes you around the dell becoming a green lane — look out for the Trust's notice and map of the site which is called Totternhoe Knolls — then down the gentle broad slope. It may not be apparent but not so long ago the fields on your left were not there, but only a bare quarry floor gleaming white with chalk. But with tons of top soil fields have been created and the 'cliffs' are mellowing.

Now stay on the greenway which curves left, ignoring the two footpaths leading off, then at the crossing where the bridleway comes up from the reconstituted quarry go sharp right. This passes by the picnic area which can be used, and enters a metalled lane which takes you out onto the road again. Bear right across the road and the stile at the footpath sign, then straight down the horse field and over the bridge. Bear left by the signs on the other side of the bridge for about 150 yards to a bridge crossing a ditch. Then a stile with a yellow arrow is found in the corner, which indicates a diagonal crossing of this field in line with the church. A fence is encountered and a stile. Do not cross, but walk alongside the fence out to the houses, which leads into a grassy lane and a gate onto the road crossed on the outgoing part of the walk. Left on the road passing the 'Bell' and the 'Old Farm Inn', turning at the tee junction by the timber-framed house, making a road return to the start point up and over a gradual hill.

Alternative return

On reaching the road at the top of Chapel Lane turn right before the fine slopes of beech trees of Castle Hill, passing the thatched and timberframed 'Cross Keys' pub which was at one time a pair of cottages. Then on to the bend in the road and enter the field by the yellow bricked house which has a footpath sign in the corner. Descend down the slope of the field staying on the left hand side through the trees and re-cross the stream, making sure you keep left at the two stiles. This brings you out into a large field. Continue with the stream by your side until a fork is met in the waters and cross over the causeway a few yards up on your right. Pass through the hedge and stay alongside the main stream taking the next footbridge. Cross the field making for yet another footbridge on the far side — these fields which are low lying can be very wet. Then keeping the fence at your side continue out up the rise into the green lane and road, then to the start as already described.

Ancient Settlements

Places included: DUNSTABLE - TOTTERNHOE - SEWELL

Length of walk: 5½ miles.

Grid Ref: Sheet 166 007214

Parking: Layby on the Whipsnade road or in Pipers Croft (2nd turning on left on Whipsnade road).

Bus services: 43, 61, 69, 245 and 343.

Public Houses: The Pheasant (West Street, Dunstable).

Walk Links: Walk 1 starts close by the parking at the bottom of the Dunstable Downs slopes. Part of Walk 2 is encountered on Castle Mound, Totternhoe, and Walk 4 at the disused railway line at Sewell.

ANCIENT SETTLEMENTS

Neolithic man left his mark by constructing round gravebarrows or 'knolls' as on Dunstable Downs. Then there are the remains of Bronze Age burials and camps as at Maiden Bower near Dunstable and Wauluds Bank in Leagrave, where tools and weapons were found by archaeologists. The Iron Age is represented by settlement on Puddle Hill, Dunstable, and the hill forts of Ravensburgh Castle on the eastern Barton Hills, possibly one on Sharpenhoe Clappers and on the summit of Ivinghoe Beacon.

On the hillsides of the north Chiltern hills can be found the remains of husbanded strips quite pronounced in many places termed lynchets; their origins range from prehistory through into the medieval period. The impact of Roman occupation is much in evidence by their building work, best seen in St Albans (Verulamium). Nothing is on the surface in Dunstable (Durocobrivis), though the existence of deep wells together with great numbers of tiles and various artefacts prove that there was an important centre around the crossroads, principally the Watling Street striding through a gap in the Chiltern Hills.

Cemeteries of the Saxon era yielded valuable jewellery and remains, whilst 'motte and bailey' fortifications at Totternhoe and Toddington and the superb churches mark the impact of the Norman dynasty.

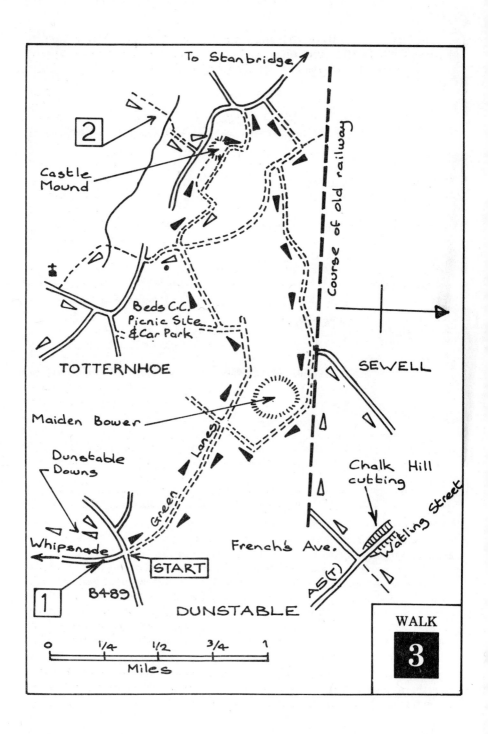

To Stanbridge

2

Castle Mound

Course of old railway

Beds C.C. Picnic Site & Car Park

TOTTERNHOE

SEWELL

Maiden Bower

Chalk Hill cutting

Dunstable Downs

Green Lanes

Whipsnade

French's Ave.

Watling Street

START

1

B489

A5(T)

DUNSTABLE

0   1/4   1/2   3/4   1
Miles

WALK
3

The foregoing hardly touches on the considerable historical remains here in the north Chiltern Hills, and when read in conjunction with the annals it soon becomes evident that this region is no historical 'backwater'.

DUNSTABLE, TOTTERNHOE, SEWELL

This is one of the walks starting from Dunstable itself and is easy going along green lanes.

The broad green lane has a belt of mature beech trees on the eastern side, bounding an area of housing including development on the old meteorological office weather station grounds. After a short distance the tree belt is left and a green lane crossing encountered, with a 'No motors' sign showing the nuisance that motorcycles can cause in the countryside. The lane on the left goes down into Totternhoe which is visited on several other walks, and we do fringe it on this one. Walk straight on, finding that the lane narrows and has some undulations; then comes a natural turn westward, for the forward direction becomes a dense hedge. What happened was that the hill's chalk was excavated by quarrying by the Totternhoe Lime and Stone Co for their lime-making — a kiln baking process — as shortly we shall see.

After some 150 yards or so of this diversion, a broad lane rising across a bare hillside is met. The great quarry is now revealed, so remember there is a sharp drop on the other side of the fence, with the floor reclaimed for agriculture by a lot of top soil, giving the realisation of just how much chalk was consumed. Compare this with the great Houghton Regis quarry whose contents became cement. A crossing of ways on the far side is passed over ignoring other side paths, then bear up the slopes slightly rightward.

A ground level water tank comes into view, then on skirting a tree lined hollow set out as a bungalow estate one is afforded views over the farm below and middle Totternhoe. The causewayed path enters the area managed by the Beds and Hunts Naturalists Society and in recent times the paths have been reconstructed. On a tree lined bend a path descends on your left side to the 'Cross Keys' and another makes a sharp right bend. Both are disregarded, for you enter the hawthorn tunnel in front, arriving on a grassy triangle at the end of an apparent field, thence across to the far end of a line of beeches straddling a ditch.

This is not a field but a bailey or outer enclosure of a Norman castle, wood built and having outer ditches still in existence. Go to the far end, then passing over other ditches you arrive on top of a mound, being the 'motte' of a 'motte and bailey' castle. Obviously the old timber posts and gateway have gone and this was never constructed in stone at a later date as with so many of the other castles in these islands, with the keep surmounting the 'motte', (Berkhamsted and Windsor). From this defensive position, by the Trig. point, tremendous views along the Chilterns are gained out to Chinnor which isn't far from the River Thames. In fact 360° viewing is obtained, even the cars coming out of the cutting on the embankment north of Dunstable can be seen.

Leave the Trig. point on the far side, taking care down the steep slopes, in the general direction of the road stretching out before you leading into Stanbridge. Then at the first stile bear hard right (NNE approx) and leave this area of the nature reserve. When reaching the corner look for a stile in about 15 yards within the hedgeline (south) taking you out into a bridleway. If you have chosen a fairweather day then mud won't be encountered. This part, twisting and turning, is reminiscent of England's old byeways, though with the occasional view of the limekilns at the works seen earlier on the castle mound (usually several can be seen firing). Eventually the way leads onto the road in front of a timber-framed house with prominent brick noggin infilling.

This is Lower End, Totternhoe, with the Eaton Bray turn-off near at hand, but we go right and right again reaching a 'Lime Kilns Only' sign at a road which we use. A slopeway which once carried a branch line for lime waggons crosses in front, though the tracks have long since gone. We pass the works entrance and before long arrive at a tee intersection of bridleways. The left takes us down to the embankment that carried the Dunstable-Leighton Buzzard railway and is an alternative loop (see map), but our direction adds more interest, for we turn right up toward the limekilns with their high loading levels and bottle shapes. The way goes on and crosses the floor of the quarry, thus providing another alternative for the return, but we go left into a hedge lined green way. This is a pleasant stretch of countryside passing an old limeworks beside the site of the railway, with the hummocks of the works and sidings now tree covered. Also we cannot escape the large opening to our right which once was a quarry, and is now partially colonised by nature though converted into agricultural usage.

The abutments of Sewell bridge come into sight, and the embankment leads into a cutting which is now a natural history reserve, but before going on our way take a closer look at Sewell and find the cottage with a sundial on the chimney stack.

Little would you realise that in this corner until quite recent times stood a crushing plant for chalk and great tanks for holding the slurry in readiness for pumping the contents to Houghton Regis and through their giant rotary kilns. (Chalk from Kensworth Quarry is crushed and the slurry pumped to Rugby!).

So on up the rise making for the beech tree belt, and round the bend in the direction of Ivinghoe Beacon on the skyline. A hedgeline around a large near circular site on the old quarry edge is just some 100 yards out in the field. This is Maidenbower of Iron Age origin and the hedgeline is on the embankment ramparts which were nearly lost at the time of the chalk workings, and strictly there is no access. Inside is a cultivated field.

In staying on the green way there is no chance of going wrong, but what is striking from this quarter is the encroachment of Dunstable into the countryside, though nowhere nearly as invasive as Luton and Houghton Regis. The crossway met on the outgoing section of the walk determines that one now retraces the first part.

Rural Skills – Strawplait and Lacemaking **4**

> **Places included:** HOUGHTON REGIS - CHALK HILL - SEWELL
>
> **Length of walk:** 4 miles.
>
> **Grid Ref:** Sheet 166 018240
>
> **Parking:** Car parks in central Houghton Regis.
>
> **Bus services:** 34, 36, 37, 38, 39, 63, 65, 75 and 652.
>
> **Public Houses:** Kings Arms (Houghton Regis)
>
> **Walk Links:** Walk 3 by the green lane near Maidenbower and the return behind Dunstable Sewerage Works forms part of Walk 5.
>
> **Notes 1:** The walk reveals the vast extent of the Portland Cement operation in Houghton Regis, though this is now a gigantic unworked quarry, the kilns having been on the southern side of the road in its working days.
>
> **2:** The route of Dunstable's projected bypass traverses this side of town, so it may have an impact on this zone.

RURAL SKILLS – STRAWPLAIT AND LACEMAKING

These cottage occupations existed for more than two centuries in the north Chiltern Hills, and whilst strawplaiting is very much a South Bedfordshire/North Herts/North Buckinghamshire activity, lacemaking could be found in Devon and Nottinghamshire besides Buckinghamshire and Bedfordshire.

Basically in strawplaiting the long straws were cut between the nodes and split into five or so slivers, then plaited into ribbons of varying widths — an occupation for all spare hands in a family. The resultant plait was pressed between wooden rollers looking very much like a miniature mangle mounted on a wall or doorframe, flattening the product, then rolled up. Entrepreneurs who delivered the straw bought the plaits, selling in the plaitmarkets of Dunstable and Luton. (Luton's old covered market was the original plait market halls). Manufacturers took the plaits and the female labour turned them into bonnets by sewing the shaped overlapping plaits on blocks. After going through several more processes the end product emerged as a Dunstable bonnet or a Luton boater.

Bobbin lacemaking on pillows was a far more intricate skill that has seen

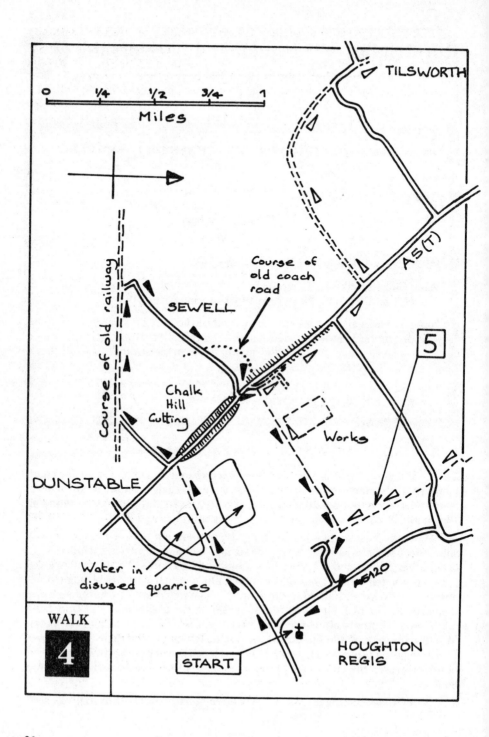

Miles

TILSWORTH

A5(T)

Course of old railway

Course of
old coach
road

SEWELL

5

Chalk
Hill
Cutting

Works

DUNSTABLE

A5120

Water in
disused quarries

WALK

4

START

HOUGHTON
REGIS

something of a revival as a pastime. Cottons wound on bobbins having beads, carvings or lovetokens, were threaded and the cottons plaited around pins stuck in a pricked card laid on a pillow which determined the pattern. The bobbins were small and several dozen had to be worked at once, hence the identification, so lace-making took an enormous amount of time. Women of the house, and it seems only women, did the work, no doubt on the grounds that men were exhausted when they returned from the fields and had not the aptitude! Women, of necessity, also did the household work and some fieldwork — gleaning and chicken-rearing, for example — so the lace-making went on into the dark night hours. The candlelight was concentrated into spots of light, shining onto the lace through water in a shaped glass container. Edgings, borders, dress-facings, shawls and cloths were made, being bought by the travelling entrepreneurs who supplied the cottons.

WALK

HOUGHTON REGIS, CHALK HILL, SEWELL

Start in the direction of Dunstable along the High Street which these days is characterless compared with years past, with so much of the housing having been replaced by factories, until you reach the Townsend Industrial Estate on the bend named after the farm here. Opposite Townsend Road is a footpath sign giving Watling Street ½ mile, located in a high hedge leading onto a concrete path between two close fences, bounded by poplars which were at one time a screen belt for the cement works. The pit on the side by the road has become a lake and, as one progresses, an even larger quarry comes into view which has become a lake at the foot of Puddle Hill. All around nature is re-colonising and one hopes that these borderlands can regenerate into countryside by colonisation. The works with their giant kilns are now a thing of the past and in fact the whole area is no longer white from dust. The path skirts the rear of the Northfields school playing fields, before arriving at the southern end of the chalk cutting.

Cross the main road here and go straight up French's Avenue, rejoining the countryside at the Sewell Cutting Nature Reserve. This disused railway cutting once carried the line into Leighton Buzzard, and the land is now under the management of the Beds and Hunts Naturalist Trust. Going through the horse barrier and making towards Sewell down the gentle incline, we can see that nature has reclaimed her land, setting trees and vegetation of all sorts into a new habitat. Leaving the reserve and embankment, on to the left hand lane, observing what was once a large chalk quarry now given a covering of topsoil and become an arable field. Make your way into Sewell, passing through the old railway bridge abutments.

Sewell is an attractive hamlet having connections with Houghton Regis. Continue along the road up to a double row of trees curving up the northern flank, being the old coach road and providing a gradual ascent of Puddle Hill in the early 1800s. The lagoons of the sewerage works come into sight and then we come out at the main road near the mouth of the cutting. Be very careful here because of the fast traffic and the blind corner. Cross just before the 'Green Man' public house and take the slip road at Chalk Hill beside the houses set against the hillside. Chalk Hill had a Methodist Chapel at one time and the steepness of the original road is very evident. Descend the slope by the houses looking for a well trodden path alongside a gable-ended house. Near a double garage, it should be signposted. Keeping left in the field beyond takes you along the southern boundary of the sewerage works, and so continue up to a ditch that seems to block your way. On close inspection a way across can be found, and the path, through a belt of undergrowth and hedging bounded by a fence on the right hand side, can be seen ahead. On the other side of the fence is a planted shelter belt of trees for a quarry expansion that never took place, as the Houghton Regis quarry closed its operational side. It is regularly walked and so the route is quite clear, then after ½ mile or so a short concrete drive is met just before a belt of trees which is the extremity of the fledgling shelter belt.

Do not go down the concrete drive but turn right and make for the path that rises up the slope in front of the trees. Then, part way up, a gap is found opening onto some waste ground and pathways in the direction of the houses. One of the paths brings you out into Rosslyn Avenue, and it now becomes a road walk until completion. Go down the Avenue into the Toddington road and then turn up the hill into Houghton, arriving in the centre by the church.

Lost Villages

Places included: HOUGHTON REGIS - CHALK HILL - TILSWORTH - HOCKLIFFE - TEBWORTH - WINGFIELD

Length of walk: 7 miles.

Grid Ref: Sheet 166 012245

Parking: The third turning on the left down Bidwell Hill on the Toddington road out of Houghton Regis is Rosslyn Avenue; go along and park on the end bend.

Bus services: 34, 36, 37, 38, 39, 63, 65, 75 and 652.

Public Houses: The Anchor (Tilsworth) and pubs in Hockliffe.

Walk Links: The path into Hockliffe is the first section of Walk 7.

LOST VILLAGES

Hockcliffe Church, as in Little Gaddesden and Kensworth, is not now the focal point of the village. Hockliffe in mediaeval times grew up around the intersection of three roads on the high ground, with the church built in the most commanding position. Although the fabric of the church dates from the 14th century, it might be on Anglo-Saxon foundations.

Houses of this era invariably do not survive, but remain as 'raised platforms' in the fields. The floor and decayed timbers and daub form recognisable house foundation shapes. Spaces can be determined between the old houses at Hockcliffe, and straight shallow ditches indicate what were once roads. This is within a radius of ¼ mile of the church, whilst outward from the fringes clear evidence of the extensive ridge and furrow field cultivation and pasturages remains.

In the course of time, as the Watling Street forming the N.E. boundary of Hockcliffe grew in importance as a drove road, so settlement increased at the roadside. By the late 16th century, cottages and inns were well established with the commencement of the travelling trade of the carters' big waggons, the forerunner of the more celebrated coaching era. This in turn attracted tradesmen over the centuries away from the church position, inevitably shrinking the life in that quarter. So it was in the 18th century, with the remaining houses around the church of this once nucleated village now known as Church End.

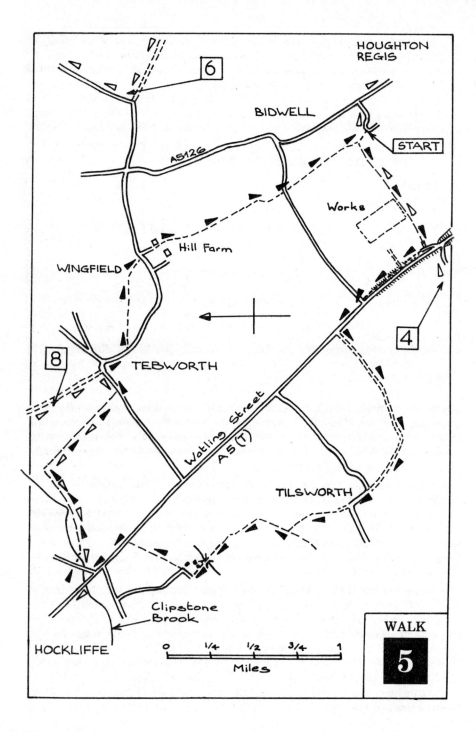

HOUGHTON REGIS

6

BIDWELL

START

A5126

Works

Hill Farm

WINGFIELD

4

8

TEBWORTH

Watling Street A5(T)

TILSWORTH

Clipstone Brook

HOCKLIFFE

0   ¼   ½   ¾   1
Miles

WALK
5

Invariably explanations can be found when tracing the loss or shrinkage of a village. Often enough one reason alone did not, and still does not, govern the fortunes of a village, for in these times buses, schools, shops, doctors and work are all key factors. Looking into the past we find such influences as soil condition, health, trade dying out, migration of population, enclosures, or land enparked and the village rebuilt nearby. In addition we have the dominance of a 'parent' village or town, causing a decline in the satellite hamlets or 'ends'. That other great influence, transport, in all its forms, has also played a major role in the success or otherwise of settlements throughout all ages.

HOUGHTON REGIS, CHALK HILL, TILSWORTH, HOCKLIFFE, TEBWORTH, WINGFIELD

WALK 5

Walking begins by going west beside the end house, making for the trees that meet up with the path. Now turn right on it and down the slope away from the housing beside a young tree belt. A concrete drive is found in front of a field. Bear sharp left here, taking the path between the tree belt and a hedgerow growing on a steep bank, for the access drive terminates at the tree belt corner. This belt was in readiness for the extension of the Houghton Regis chalk quarrying which did not materialise.

There is no mistaking where to go, for the first part utilises this no-man's-land, then on encountering a much-reduced-in-size hedge in front, get across into the field and make for the corner at your right hand side. It entails negotiating one or two ditches. This field may be in arable or in crop, but it becomes the southern limit of the Dunstable Sewage Works and the path is always here. On a bit more and the path enters a passageway between gardens, joining the old Chalk Hill road. Here we are on the old course of the Watling Street, and a hamlet, with its own Methodist church, community and turnpike road (also the detour for horse-drawn coaches) is found in the trees behind the 'Green Man' public house.

From above you, on the tree covered embankment, comes the roar of traffic bound for Dunstable, but our direction is down the slope on the metalled surface. Then proceed, still against the embankment, along a grassy lane when the road goes toward the sewerage works. This is passable until it peters out, and the field boundary now becomes the path, while the embankment drops almost to field level. Then by skirting the corner a gap can be found giving easy access onto the Thorn road. Now, unfortunately, the main road must be used for a short distance along the grass verge on the same side. Find the 5th lamp-post on the opposite side of the A5, and a substantial farm drive becomes evident through a tree gap by the roadside, but be very careful when crossing. Before leaving notice that it is in fact a double line of trees and hedges, for here is the true course of the Watling Street, one of Britain's greatest Roman roads.

Very easy walking now, with a good vantage of Puddle Hill and its cutting, while the coachroad of 1782 rises across the brow and passes across the Sewell road. By the bridleway sign this substantial track bears right and makes for the village of Tilsworth, coming out on the remnant village green.

Keep straight forward when the road heads off in the Leighton Buzzard direction. We pass close by some country cottages in this quarter, then using the gate enter a narrow field. Up and through another small gate, and in staying with this grassy depression we find that the slope begins levelling out and a gate is discovered. Cross this field carefully, whatever is growing there, in a straight line on the same course, and meet up with a corner of low hedges on the end of a track — don't be worried as this path is on the maps.

Change direction eastward and use the same stretch as in the Eggington walk, as repeated here. In the same alignment as the left hand track strike out across this large field, even though there are no distinguishing landmarks, then as the ground starts falling away bear slightly left in the direction of a grazing meadow nearest you. As you get nearer, a small pedestrian gateway can be seen in the fencing leading you into the meadow seen from the hilltop. Once inside, stay against the left hand hedgerow, and on reaching the recently constructed stile, cross and follow the hedge in a north-westerly direction. Exit by another new stile and cross this meadow, making for the trees in front of some bungalows. Here a bridge over a brook brings you to the rear of the end bungalow. Turn sharp left and follow the L.H. tree line between two wire fences where there should be a stile followed by one on the outlet. Cross over some grass and enter an animal enclosure keeping to the left and join the road by crossing a five-barred gate. This is an officially diverted path not yet shown on O.S. maps and marked by a signpost. Right on the road for a short distance and at the corner take the path crossing the large field here with a scattering of trees as a landmark. On down to the main road at the stream's bridge.

Left into Hockliffe and leave on the Woburn road by turning right at the crossroads. Just past the Dick Whittington cattery, the last property on the right, go over the stile and between the trees, traverse the footbridge, bringing you out into a long meadow. In fact this section is the reverse of part of the route of the Battlesden-Tebworth walk. One can either stay with the banks of the Clipstone Brook or make for the distant gate and the one beyond, staying this time by the right hand hedges as you must do in the third field. Nearly at the end of this particular field an open gateway comes into sight. Pass through and directly across this field through the gateway, and make for a clump of trees slightly right in the opposite hedge.

This proves to be at the end of a paddock adjoining a very large arable field. Cross the barbed wire into the trees, and sharp right into the field getting over some more wire. Actually this is not as difficult as it sounds. Now, keeping alongside the treeline on your left, walk up the slope. In the lower parts there might not be much space in the headlands when crops are growing, but on leaving the overhead gridline this opens into a wide grassy width which is much better. The road is gained, so left into the village, looking at the houses and noting their features before thinking of departing.

We leave on the Wingfield road, then just as the timberyard is left, a footpath sign for Wingfield stands in a field corner on the other side of the road. Leave the road, taking a diagonal direction right across the field through the crop that leaves the rear of the roadside houses (you will find that it goes for the left hand end of a row of farm outbuildings). On the skyline left is the profile of Toddington church, then some frail fencing shows us into a horsefield. Through this one and the one after, both usually well grazed. Some housing comes into sight, and by taking the single plank bridge enter a rough pasture area. The quite discernable path works its way along the gardens between boundaries into Wingfield itself.

Turn left and make for the 'Festival of Britain 1951' village sign, as found throughout Bedfordshire in the villages commemorating the 100th anniversary of the 1851 Great Exhibition in Hyde Park built by William Paxton — Bedfordshire's famous gardener.

But to continue; right down the no-through road alongside the cricket field toward Hill Farm, but look out for the period farm on your right before going too far. Pass through the gate with the recently built cottages on the left, and go forward to the outer limit of the farmhouse grounds with the house to your left and buildings at your right. Having walked directly forward from the gate, Houghton Regis stands clearly on the skyline hill.

Bear slightly left and descend the slope, keeping this hedge on your right hand side round a bulge of rough ground to the field's end. Drop down into the dry ditch on your right and go under the cross hedge in the tee junction — very easy really. Follow the left hedge skirting the pylon, eventually passing through a rough meadow and its unkempt tree-lined pond in the meadow, close by a piece of dense woodland, then out by the gate onto the road.

A lot of traffic at times here, but use the road left onto the bend and take the path in the gap across the road. It crosses the field, on a grass causewayed clearway with cultivation on both sides. Arriving at the brook go left on the farm bridge and carry on right into the next field having turned 180°. We change direction again and stay close by the hedgerow on our left on a clearly defined bridleway/footpath up the slope of the land in the direction of Houghton Regis.

After a while it disappears round a bend into some woodland onto a concrete drive. This we take, but instead of going into the wood, we stay right on the drive beside the field. On turning at the top we realise that this is the self-same drive seen soon after the start of the walk. Return to the commencement diagonally up across the rough open ground on the other side of the trees which define the path.

Habitats

Places included: HOUGHTON REGIS - CHALTON

Length of walk: 4 miles.

Grid Ref: Sheet 166 035 259

Parking: Off the road in the vicinity of the start, spaces can be found.

Bus services: 23 & 24 routes go into Chalton, and the walk can then commence there. Otherwise buses 37 & 38 into Houghton Regis. Buses do not pass the start.

Public Houses: The Harvest Home (Houghton Regis), The Star and The Fancott Arms (Chalton).

Walk Links: From Wingfield on Walk 5 by road crossing the A5120 to Toddington down minor road to New Barn Farm. Also, Houghton Regis/Sundon Road has cross links (see Ordnance Survey map).

HABITATS

Habitats for flora and wildlife are more diverse than might be expected, in addition to the usual fields, hedges and woodlands.

Increasingly roadside verges play a role, with the highway authorities showing consideration both in their cutting programmes for the promotion of indigenous flora and by seeding with low maintenance grasses mixed with wildflower seed. Railway and motorway fringes are acknowledged natural sites, whether by the process of colonising or deliberate tree planting and seeding. Regenerative countryside can be seen in the worked-out quarries, particularly the Houghton Regis quarry. In addition this one has open stretches of water which are a lung for north Dunstable, whilst the attendant rushes are a stopover for waterfowl.

In the countryside fallen timber becomes a home for fungi and insects during its decay, all part of nature's food-chain. Sometimes wood is gathered and stacked for this purpose. Rural churchyards and cemeteries of venerable age furnish a home for a bewildering range of life, especially the mosses and lichens. Stone built church walls and gravestones can appear to insects as a miniature quarry with its own microclimate, being on the damp side if evergreens are planted nearby and harbouring rare plants. East Anglian villagers make a point of tending their ecclesiastical grounds and thereby

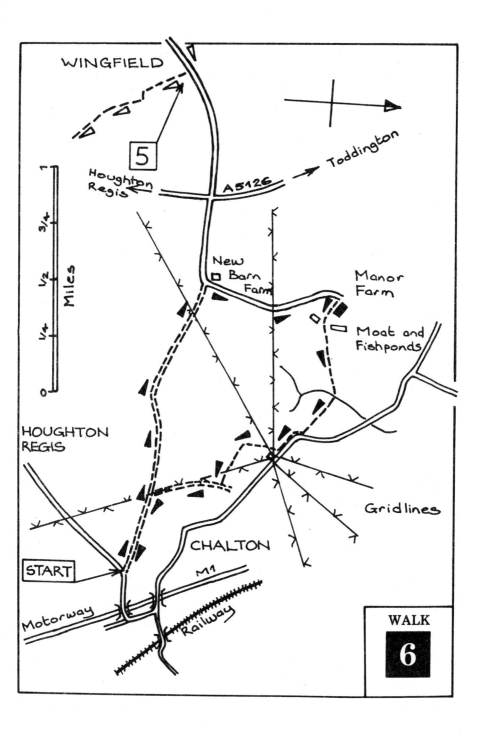

WINGFIELD

5

Houghton
Regis

A5126 → Toddington

New
Barn
Farm

Manor
Farm

Moat and
Fishponds

1
3/4
1/2
Miles
1/4
0

HOUGHTON
REGIS

Gridlines

CHALTON

START

M1

Motorway

Railway

WALK

6

controlling the grass mowing timetables, protecting orchids and meadowland flowers, such places being their last sanctuaries.

Only by grazing can the springy downland turf be maintained by sheep and rabbits, giving the finer grasses a chance in the sward. Sheep reintroduced on the Barton Hills are paying dividends for the flora, while providing an income for the farmers. The possibility of bringing sheep back onto Dunstable Downs is under consideration.

With so many natural ponds lost for ever in the countryside by disuse, by infilling, and because of the lowered watertable, the humble garden pond is increasingly asssuming importance as a haven for amphibians. And we need not stop there, for by planting bushes such as the buddleia we are contributing to the butterfly food supply. Modern gardening books devote a chapter to plants that attract butterflies and other animals. Whilst on the subject of habitats, television provides programmes for the armchair naturalists about the urban foxes and sometimes badgers just outside their windows. The animal world must adapt with man or perish, unless we help their natural surroundings.

WALK

HOUGHTON REGIS, CHALTON

The green lane we use is in fact part of an alignment stretching from Lilley and in the other direction Wingfield, as a look at the map will show, and acts as a link for several walks.

There are no difficulties in this stretch, as it is simply a matter of staying on the bridleway, passing under a major gridline near the beginning. This section is something like 1½ miles long. Then, just after passing Grove Farm and a small wood and under a second gridline, New Barn Farm is met. It is on the corner where the Chalgrave Manor road comes up from the Toddington road.

Take this road, and after leaving a small wood belt at your left hand side, the Manor comes into view, so stay on the road right up to the farm itself. Now enter the field in front of the farmhouse by the gate in the corner near a tree, then stay by the left hand fence in the direction of a wood-belt at the field boundary. Notice the moats, or what could possibly have been fishponds in late manorial times, but look for the gap between the ponds and cross over the next field heading away from the farm. Now comes the only real difficulty on the walk, but there is a landmark that helps identification.

On leaving the ponds you should be on the left of a hedgerow stretching out in the general direction of a white tower on the distant hill — the landmark. You will find that you will be bearing slightly left. Go over the tubular steel gate and the next field, coming upon a ditch, the crossing of which is usually reasonably manageable. Now you should see three solitary trees out in a large field — a sure sign of a missing hedge — and use this as a guide, coming out onto the bend of the Fancott/Chalton road.

Instead of using the road for the next section, it is much better that the field alongside is walked, staying close by the roadside hedge and meeting up with a group of pylon towers in the corner. Now stay in this field and keep close by a left hand hedge which has many bends, then one looks out for a small bridge as a means of traversing a fairly wide ditch. Stay by this field's boundary, then on arriving at the fence, at a suitable point enter the lane which is a farm access drive.

For the return, turn right going uphill on the fringe of Chalton, following the line of an overhead grid coming out onto the greenlane, and it is simply a matter of retracing the beginning.

Watery Defences

Places included: HOCKLIFFE - EGGINGTON - STANBRIDGE - TILSWORTH

Length of walk: 4 miles.

Grid Ref: Sheet 165 975265

Parking: Birch's Close housing estate first on right approaching Hockliffe from the south.

Bus services: 69, 139, 268 and 545.

Public Houses: The Anchor (Tilsworth), The Red Lion (Tilsworth), Five Bells of Stanbridge, pubs in Hockliffe. The Horseshoes (Eggington).

Walk Links: Walk 5 crosses through the start point of this walk, and Walk 8 can be met at the Woburn Road junction in the middle of Hockliffe.

Notes: 1. On the high ground approaching Eggington there are some very fine long distance views, and the fields around here used for sheep grazing.

2. The walk does not actually pass Tilsworth Manor and its moat, so a short diversion or adaptation of the walk is necessary.

3. Eggington village is worth visiting, having a charm of its own, and keep a look out for the brick tower of Stanbridge windmill (see notes for Walk 2.)

WATERY DEFENCES

Moated manors and farms are surprisingly common in this area, signifying the availability of clay for puddling the lining of the waterway, just as the canals were 'puddled' a few centuries later in order that a supply of water was on hand or could be diverted.

Quite a number of moated sites appear on the Ordnance Survey maps, some now only ditches, whilst several were complete watercourses. As a result of subsequent back-filling, moats cannot be found except for lush growth on rich

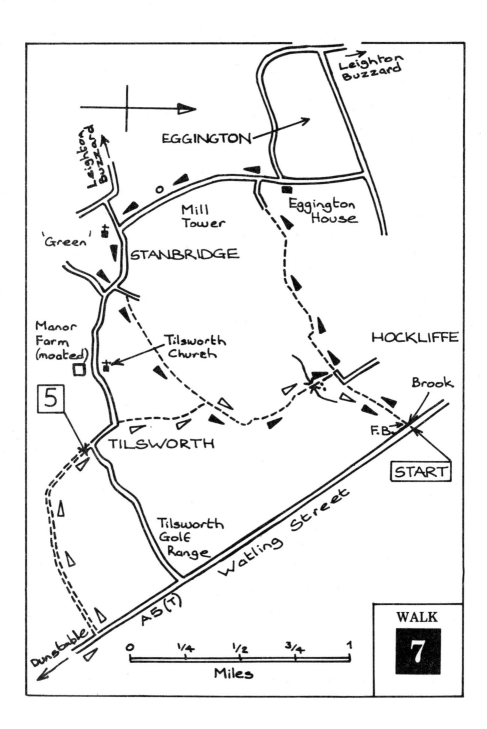

Leighton Buzzard

EGGINGTON

Leighton Buzzard

Mill Tower

'Green'

STANBRIDGE

Eggington House

Manor Farm (moated)

Tilsworth Church

HOCKLIFFE

Brook

5

F.B.

START

TILSWORTH

Tilsworth Golf Range

Watling Street

A5(T)

Dunstable

0   1/4   1/2   3/4   1

Miles

WALK

7

damp soils or aerial photographs showing crop-marks. Yet they are recorded on old estate maps.

It would appear that the construction of moats around manor houses and farmsteads was fashionable rather than functional as a first line of defence in later years. The plain of Aylesbury (as in the flat lands of East Anglia), in the absence of stone for defence walling, adopted moats. As another example crenellations were added for effect rather than fortification after the introduction of cannons.

Usually moated sites are on the low lands, and a glance at the map reveals a relatively large number. These include Chalton Manor, Thorn, Tilsworth, Eaton Bray, Edlesborough, Wilstone (Gubblecote), Buckland, Aston Clinton (2), Hulcott (Aylesbury), Drayton Beauchamp, Apsley End (2) (NE Barton) and another in Barton.

By researching on the ground and in archival material more sites can be found; the nationally recognised Moated Sites Research Group keeps files of field cards but they do not include mediaeval castle moats.

HOCKLIFFE, EGGINGTON, STANBRIDGE, TILSWORTH

Near the pedestrian crossing at the southern end of Hockliffe is a footbridge over a stream. It has a footpath sign by the railings and acts as the start and finish.

Cross the bridge and go directly away from the road towards a scattering of trees on the brow ahead, and since the path is always trodden out through the crops there is no difficulty, and it is an officially marked path. After the trees keep on the way, making for a hedgerow in front of some bungalows. This brings you out on the corner of a road. Take the road for a short distance until it ceases at a metal gate. Pass through, taking the trackway up to the pigfarm, rising all the time. Then almost at the buildings go over the right hand fence into the field, being careful to avoid any nettles. It is anti-clockwise around the farm, so follow the adjacent fence until a crossing is found between two closely growing trees. Skirt round the buildings with their scattering of old vehicles and implements — why does one find so much unused stock at farms? Plain walking now on the right hand of the hedgerow along the ridge, with good views of Hockliffe church on the far rise through the fields. After about half a mile switch to the left hand side at a convenient point on the slight bend of the hedgerow. This new side presents no difficulties as one walks on either the headland or grass depending upon the uses of the fields, which in this area are usually for sheep grazing.

A double planked bridge crossing a ditch is encountered with some fencing (you are on the wrong side of the hedge if you don't), and the path gets wider, bearing leftward, coming eventually into a lane which takes the walker onto the Eggington road. A walk through the village is worth the extra effort now you are here, as being tucked away it almost escapes notice. Many buildings are several hundred years old and eyecatching. Standing in a commanding position above is Eggington House, having a classical Queen Anne facade and finials on the parapet, in all an imposing edifice.

Resuming the walk unfortunately necessitates using the road to Stanbridge, though it is never busy and provides high views out to the west. One soon passes the tower of Eggington windmill, now converted into a residence, and descends into Stanbridge. The church is before you, and the fair-sized village green in front of the church is a good stopping point for a rest on the seats.

Turn left onto the Tilsworth road passing the infants' school and on to the bend in the road. Then left into Kings Way a hundred yards or so down the slope beside a high hedge. Look out for the footpath sign indicating a narrow grassy path between the houses, then pass over a couple of closely positioned stiles and bear left into an L-shaped field making diagonally for the corner hedge. Continue parallel to the Tilsworth road and them I am afraid it is a bit of a fight to get out at the far end. Maybe the council can one day be persuaded to reinstate the stile, as it is part of a walk. We are now in a corner of a big field disappearing across the hilltop, but we stay against the right hand fence above the local playing field diverging away from Tilsworth itself. A track comes up from the village church turning in front of you and becomes a path which abruptly stops at a remnant hedge.

Do not be deterred by the field in front in spite of its large size and the possible absence of a recognisable path, as it can be in crop or ploughed and there are no distinguishing landmarks. The advice is to stay on the same alignment up onto the brow and pass downward in a slightly leftward direction towards the corner of a grazing meadow nearest you. As you get nearer a small pedestrian gateway can be seen in the fencing which takes you into the meadow seen from the distance. Once inside stay against the left hand hedgerow, and on reaching the recently constructed stile, cross and follow the hedge in a north-westerly direction.

Exit by another new stile and cross this meadow making for the trees in front of the bungalows seen on the way out; at their rear a bridge is discovered and crossed. Turn sharp left and follow the L.H. tree line between two wire fences where there should be a stile followed by one on the outlet. Cross over some grass and enter an animal enclosure keeping to the left and join the road by a five-barred gate. Actually this is the officially diverted path though not shown re-routed on O.S. maps and has a signpost for proof.

Right on the road down to the corner and retrace the outgoing path.

Farmbuilding Evolution

Places included: HOCKLIFFE - BATTLESDEN - TEBWORTH

Length of walk: 6 miles.

Grid Ref: Sheet 165 966270

Parking: Around the edge of the triangular green in front of the church.

Bus services: 69, 139, 268 and 545.

Public Houses: Hockliffe pubs. The Queen's Head (Tebworth).

Walk Links: Walk 7 starts at the southern end of Hockliffe, and Walk 5 is met on the Tebworth/Hockliffe return.

FARMBUILDING EVOLUTION

Farming evolution continues unabated with a concentration at this end of the 20th century on machinery, chemicals, yields, specialisations, bigger fields and finance.

Centre Farm (in Battlesden) which is of the Georgian pattern, known also as a Hanoverian (George I to George IV) or model farm, dominates this walk as the key feature. A word or two about farm developments to amplify the topic.

Lord 'Turnip' Townsend and Thomas Coke of Holkham Hall, Norfolk, experimented in crop rotation, the introduction of root crops, draining, manuring, sowing, breeding livestock and feeding. Attention was given to the design and usage of the farmbuildings themselves in relation to these developments. Silage, oilcake and rootcrops meant that cattle could now be wintered, not slaughtered en masse as in the past.

Linked barns around stockyards proved very functional, but farms were of the mixed farming variety aiming for self sufficiency, so provision for thrashing and grain storage was naturally included. Developments in wagons and implements meant that these capital intensive pieces of equipment required their own sheds, besides thinking about providing nearby accommodation for stockmen and keyworkers.

Centre Farm, being of brick of the 18th going into the 19th century, besides being functional is also aesthetically pleasing.

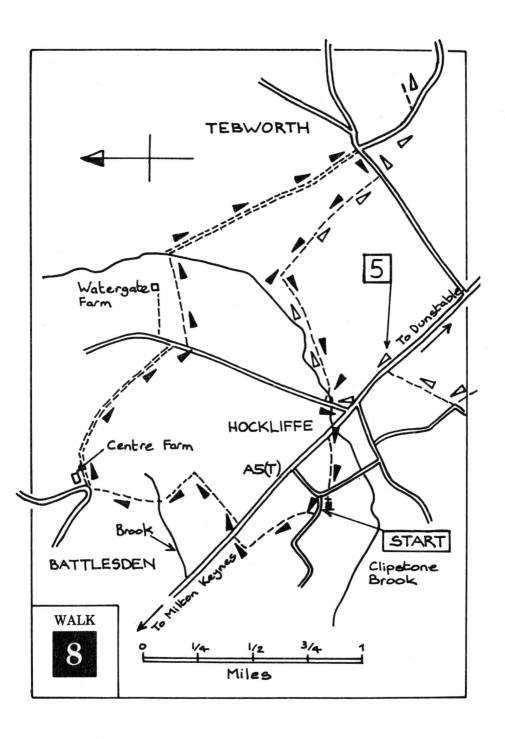

TEBWORTH

5

To Dunstable

Watergate Farm

HOCKLIFFE

To Dunstable

Centre Farm

A5(T)

START

Brook

Clipstone Brook

BATTLESDEN

To Milton Keynes

WALK

8

0   1/4   1/2   3/4   1

Miles

43

HOCKLIFFE, BATTLESDEN, TEBWORTH

Park at the triangular green in front of the church, and before you is a tidy thatched cottage with partial 'cruck' timber framing. Views stretch out in a north-easterly direction from this high ground.

Leave by taking the road up the right hand side of the church and look out for the stile just before the bend on the north side. The field is very hummocky, reputed to be the site of the old village with the bumps of the decayed houses, for as will be observed, the new village is now along the A5 and not around the church. From here onwards Leighton Buzzard with its soaring church spire can clearly be seen in the distance, but the way is on the right of the field in the tree line. Stay on the boundary even when there are right angled bends.

In a corner of the fencing is a stile, though the footboard is missing. Cross the field and proceed alongside the allotments to what appears to be a tunnel in a hedgerow. Actually you will find this is really an overgrown gateway and heavily fenced, so look about for a suitable gap in the hedge, which may mean walking a few yards in the direction of Hockliffe searching for an access point. Descend very carefully onto the path at the roadside, bearing in mind that this is a busy fast road, and go south for about 100 yards or so looking for a gateway on the other side of the road.

Cross the road, then over the iron gate, rising up the slope into the open field system. Go forward alongside the left hand sheep mesh fencing. As you go on, Dunstable is clearly seen to the south from the high ground here. Watch out for livestock and keep dogs under control, as this is working farmland. On reaching the hedge enter the left hand field through the detachable fencing and re-close, then follow the boundary past a water trough. (The diagonal bridleway shown on the Ordnance Survey map is effectively diverted, becoming two sides of a triangle).

On reaching the tree line go through or over the gate and make sure it is closed because of the livestock. A stream is shown on the map and is usually dry, with the ditch at the foot of the trees. Bearing right take the old path alignment and pass across the brow with the white painted Hill Farm as a marker. By following the left hand hedge in these fields, go out by the gate alongside a stream. Battlesden can now be seen as a hamlet, though the church is well away from these houses. With tree planting close at hand the reinstating of trees is a healthy sign. Another gate, and on the bridleway between a pair of fences, then bear left up the slope into Battlesden.

Look out for one of Bedfordshire's 1951 Festival of Britain village nameboards and the rather murky pond. Sharp right on the bend of the road, passing at the side of Centre Farm with its Georgian 'model' farm buildings. These are a range of buildings, yards and barns set out with specific functions as sheds for storage, livestock, implements etc., as described in books about the history of farming. You are now on a gated road with livestock grazing in the area, so be careful to keep dogs on a leash. However the going is very easy, affording views from this relatively high vantage ground.

So on down to the B528. Right at the road for a few yards, looking out for a stile in the hedgerow on the other side of the road, then stay by this hedge beside the 18th century Watergate Farm with its 19th century additions. Climb over the stapled footgate, and on down to Clipstone Brook, crossing by means of the bridge, but don't hurry on. The brook joins the River Ouzel in Leighton Buzzard and is most attractive at this point, with the overhanging trees making a birdlife habitat. So wait and listen to the sound of running water and birdsong.

The broad lane which eventually leads into Tebworth cannot be mistaken. The hedges retain many trees and new ones are encouraged — a healthy practice. Having a good surface it serves as an access for all the neighbouring fields. There is a rise into Tebworth, which retains much of its vernacular old buildings, with some converted in a sympathetic manner into dwellings — do your own spotting. Personally I think it is worth wandering round the whole village before resuming with the last stage of the walk, for the buildings in a distinctive red brick conform to the nucleated pattern, with each playing a role in former days.

Leave the village on the Hockliffe road and stop at the last house on your right hand side on the boundary corner. Enter the very large field, which usually has a grassy broad headland, and follow the hedgerow down the slope under the grid system until halted at the far corner. Simply cross the right hand fence under the trees and immediately left over the adjacent fence into a long grazing meadow. Cross over, making for the open gateway in the opposite hedgerow, then cross the next field, heading for a gate normally kept closed, in the hedge. If these notes are not abided by, time is wasted in tramping around boundary hedges. In these and the next fields watch out for livestock.

Through the gate and reclose it, and sharp left through the long narrow meadows meeting up with the Clipstone Brook again, serpenting along with teasles growing on its banks. Eventually you are funnelled into the right hand end corner of the meadow under a canopy of trees, which reveal a footbridge and path by the Whittington Cattery on the Woburn road crossed earlier.

Left into Hockliffe and at the traffic lights right in the direction of Milton Keynes on the A5 looking out for the former village hall a few hundred yards up from the lights on the other side of the road. Alongside is a footpath sign which is your return, taking the stile at the rear of the hall into grazing fields with rather a lot of thistles. Make your way up the slopes in the direction of the church, but aiming for the left hand end of the row of cottages before you, and a footpath sign by a stile becomes visible. Out onto the road and along to the green triangle outside the church boundary wall.

Villages and their Greens

Places included: UPPER SUNDON - FANCOTT - TODDINGTON

Length of walk: 5 miles.

Grid Ref: Sheet 166 045278

Parking: In Common Lane behind The Crown PH.

Bus services: 22. Alternatively, use the 24 into Toddington and use the walk as a circular to Upper Sundon or stop short at the motorway.

Public Houses: The Crown (Upper Sundon), The Fancott Arms (Fancott), public houses around the green in Toddington.

Walk Links: Road link between Fancott and Chalton for Walk 6. The start of Walk 10 is on the Harlington road out of Upper Sundon.

Notes 1: The footbridge over the railway is a good position for train-spotters; also the actual size of the Toddington M1 service area really becomes apparent from the bridges.

2: One cannot help but be amazed by the complexity of the grid power lines converging on the Chalton site.

VILLAGES AND THEIR GREENS

A number of places in the area have names ending with -ington. Very loosely, the 'ing' implies 'the people of' Cadd or Todd and the 'ton' denotes settlement, possibly with some basic defence even if only an enclosure safeguarding cattle. If 'ham' is on the end of the name then a home or steading is denoted (hamlet). Spellings of place names change over the centuries, so the prefix can have its own long history and become much corrupted. As an example, Eaton (Eton) indicates watermeadows or lees (fields which were deliberately flooded), thus increasing the soil fertility by alluvium deposits. The second part of a place name is often a surname, as in deBray, Conquest, Gobion, Ferrers to name but a few, with the suffix Regis always showing royal connections.

Villages with greens predominate mainly in the east and north-east of England where a case can be made for tracing their development as cattle enclosures against rustling and spoils.

But villages and their greens cannot be neatly pigeon-holed. They have been

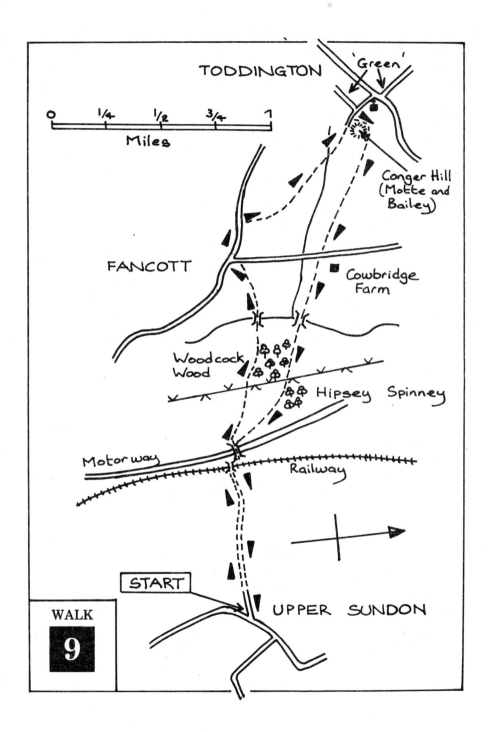

TODDINGTON

'Green'

Conger Hill
(Motte and
Bailey)

0   ¼   ½   ¾   1
Miles

FANCOTT

Cowbridge
Farm

Woodcock
Wood

Hipsey Spinney

Motorway

Railway

START

UPPER SUNDON

WALK

9

eroded by many causes, not least by main roads crossing them. Should a village develop in a linear form as plots along a roadway, no normal green results, and we have a 'street village'; when growth radiates from a central open space the term 'green village' gets used; close compact form gives a 'nucleated village'. There are also those without recognisable form, possibly originating as clusters of squatter huts, farms and random housing.

Toddington satisfies what has become the pre-requisite of a typical village in having a green with housing around the perimeter, a church on one side and a water supply. Finchingfield, that much photographed village in Essex, also conforms.

Greens may be sited away from the church when grazing and geese feature in village affairs, or as a place for moots, gatherings, festivities, fairs and travelling salesmen of all descriptions. Social history researchers generally agree that the 'green' did not come into the influence of the church, and by custom only a smithy, school, and sometimes a moot hall might be granted permission for the erection of a permanent building within the boundaries of the green.

Encroachment over the centuries proved inevitable with houses, trades, and farm buildings vying for space, then there are the cultivation pressures from market gardeners, orchards and allotments. And so many villages no longer have greens or only an irregular small patch. Speculating on the origins of greens, we have the wide spaced hedgerows of the drove roads, 'in-fields', demesne land, fragments from the old mediaeval great field rotations, and unproductive agricultural lands. To this day there is a society that is solely concerned with commons and open spaces.

WALK

UPPER SUNDON, FANCOTT, TODDINGTON

Proceed past the housing in the first part of Common Lane until it becomes a pathway and joins the made-up road servicing landfill at the Sundon cement works' quarries, with the buildings now demolished and nature regaining the barren land. We come into an area which is a terrible eyesore of rubbish-dumping along the approach to the footbridge over the railway (London St Pancras - Bedford and the North), which leads on toward the M1 motorway bridge and a path left down a ramp onto the fields.

Away on the left is the immense switchyard of the gridsystem, then in front is a path crossing the field and passing to the left of a pylon with some fenced-off insulators at its foot. Use this path up to the next hedgerow – labels show the system is 132 KV overhead. It is noticed that a line of powerlines on wooden poles traverses the next two fields, and since the fields are mostly under arable farming the correct route is straight through, for the farmer does not reinstate this particular path. Take the tree cables as a line of sight. (Strictly, going around the outside of the field is trespassing). Just to the left of where the cables pass across the main hedgerow is a footbridge of concrete with handrails in very good condition, but it may be out of sight because of undergrowth. Pass into the field and make for the rather delapidated pair of pedestrian gates which must be kept shut (or they fall down!), because of cattle. Then walk up along the right hand hedgerow and out onto the road by crossing the corner fence.

At the roadside is an enclosed yard of service gas valves on your left. These are passed as you approach the tee junction, with the well known 'Fancott Arms' down on the left hand bend of the road. Sharp right up the road past White Hart Farm, looking out for the footpath sign on the bend of the road near at hand. Cross over the road and enter the field, making for the upper hedge line, and after about two or three hundred yards a gateway is found. Climb over and Toddington church should be visible on the skyline. The way is now slightly bearing right through cattle gates and over fences into a field which has a gate out into a wooded lane at its far end. At this watercourse crossing there is a stile, the pathway alongside the brook enters a country lane. This end of Toddington contains attractive thatched and timber framed houses. In a short distance, past the Conger Lane bus garage, one arrives on the Green in Toddington, a village well worth exploring.

Back to the bus garage in Conger Lane for the commencement of the return route. Look for the kissing-gate nearby leading into a sheep grazing field. You cannot miss the great mound in the centre which is Conger Hill, where witches are supposed to make their pancakes on Shrove Tuesday – inside of course. In fact it is the motte of a castle with its encircling ditch, with the bailey or castle yard apparently on the southern side, for there is a well-defined perimeter ditch in places.

Leave by the far gate which is alongside the cemetery boundary hedge, and pass into the open fields where the hills of Barton and surrounding area show up on the left horizon. The track is easy to follow and the going is good, with high elevations over the motorway and the nearby Toddington service station, which from this height covers a bigger area than expected. After a while the track becomes a path which down towards the road at the foot is not distinguishable, but just stay by the left hand hedgerow, or what is left of it, and there is no difficulty. On arriving onto the road turn right and walk the short distance to the drive leading to the side of Cowbridge Farm. You cannot miss the drive as there is white fencing by the roadside.

Pass into the field in front and stay on the boundary track against the hedge, which takes you to a concrete crossing of the stream. Then in front is a ditch which leads to the wood on the slopes where there was once a hedgerow; go up on the left side of this drainage ditch.

Pass alongside this woodland, named Woodcock Wood, which we saw on the outgoing section, and over the brow of the rise. Ahead we see the motorway and gain a closer view of the Toddington Services, realising what a considerable area it covers. Again the hedge line is missing, with only a few remaining trees to show the alignment, so we continue straight over, arriving beside Hipsey Spinney which we follow on its southern side. Stop at the far corner, for in fact you will find the field completely encircles the Spinney. Look around for a fence, beyond which is the sloping path down from the motorway footbridge used earlier.

As you can see two fields must be traversed to get to the objective whether corn is growing or not, so set yourself on alignmment and make the crossing.

Naturally the return from now onwards is the same as the outgoing, but watch for the footpath on the left hand side which leaves the road and leads into Common Lane – you can miss it.

Spare that Tree and Plant One More

Places included: UPPER SUNDON - SHARPENHOE AND STREATLEY AREA

Length of walk: 5 miles.

Grid Ref: Sheet 166 046288

Parking: Adequate parking in the Bedfordshire County Council car park.

Bus services: 22 for Upper Sundon, 78 for Streatley.

Public Houses: The Chequers (Streatley), The Lynmore (Sharpenhoe).

Walk Links: The start of Walk 9 can be easily reached by road in Upper Sundon. A road walk of 1½ miles from Sharpenhoe into Barton in the Clay brings you onto the turning point of Walk 11 by the church.

Notes 1: There is an excellent picnic area provided at the car park.

2: A useful map of the Sundon Hills Country Park is mounted on posts at the car park entrance, and a further pictorial map can be found on the pathway leading to Sharpenhoe Clappers.

3: The walk can be done in its entirety or just taken as a stroll around the Sharpenhoe Clappers using the Streatley to Sharpenhoe road. Another alternative is for some to commence the walk in Sundon and the driver to take the car around to the Clappers park.

4: This is termed a Chilterns Area of Outstanding Natural Beauty, so please take every care, and if dogs are taken on the walk beware of disturbing sheep. Sharpenhoe Clappers is a National Trust site.

SPARE THAT TREE AND PLANT ONE MORE

Replenished either by natural regeneration or by planting schemes, trees are an indispensable part of the English countryside. Any government policies abetting hedgerow and woodland destruction by the farming world must stop, and strict sanctions and reviewing procedures be instituted. This headlong destruction of woodland is a worldwide phenomenon, as is happening in Amazonia, for example.

Nature's indomitable tenacity begins reclaiming open spaces if at all possible, though often this exceeds a man's lifetime. In the disused chalk

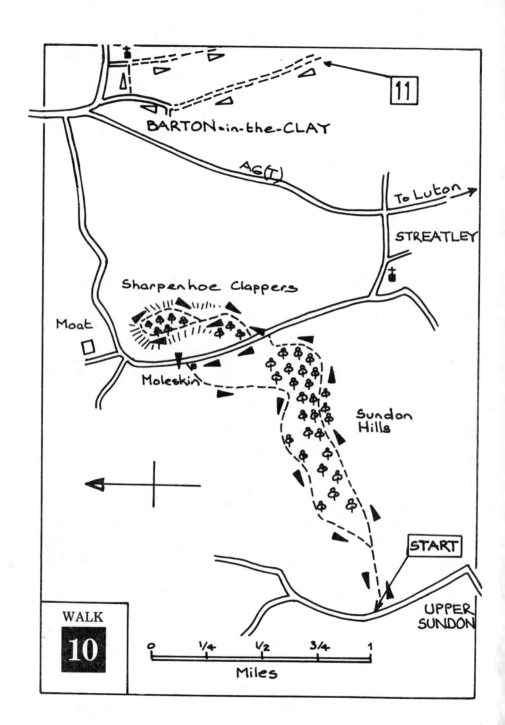

BARTON-in-the-CLAY

A6(T)

To Luton

STREATLEY

Sharpenhoe Clappers

Moat

Moleskin

Sundon Hills

START

UPPER SUNDON

11

WALK

10

0   ¼   ½   ¾   1

Miles

quarries the process can be observed, beginning with a covering of lichens starting a cycle of humous creation. This traps windblown dust and grasses, coltsfoot and the like, and prepares the way for arboreal colonising. Birch appears first, then sallow willow, and with footholds gained, oaks, ash, sycamores and some beech establish, if fortunate, in the increasing ground mulch.

For nearly 5,000 years the trees of Europe developed in the changing climates. Nowadays they hang on relatively precariously against man, not regaining vigour in many areas because sheep graze out the young saplings and shoots on the uplands. This century has seen extensive planting of various cash-cropping conifers, arousing dismay that the indigenous deciduous species are not featuring greatly. Little of the primeval woodland survives.

The sight of trees maturing in the hedgerows is another familiar aspect of the countryside, for hedges can be more than ten centuries old, first set as manorial boundaries. Or they can be remnant survivors of great woodlands, but usually they were planted as quicksets during the enclosures, with hazel, blackthorn, elderberry and rowan finding a habitat, besides fledgling trees taking root from seed. Along roadsides holly was set, delineating the lanes in time of heavy snowfalls. The Chilterns are renowned for their beechwoods, especially around High Wycombe (valley of the Chilterns' River Wye), whilst here in the northern hills there is still a good representation of woodland, as discovered on many of the walks.

Amongst old English words, assart, riding, laundes and worth, all indicate clearance of woodland for cultivation or settlement, whilst field or feld meant an open space in an otherwise forested area. In considering nomenclature, the words clappers and warren are both used for rabbit-rearing places, supplying the lord's table.

Names used for the right of collecting wood a few centuries back yield several unfamiliar words, viz. hedgebote – stakes and the likes for fencing; housebote – wood for house repairs; whilst firebote, naturally, simply stood for firewood fuel. Furze appears in records for brackens, heathplants and brushwood for bedding and for firing brickclamps and kilns.

WALK

UPPER SUNDON, SHARPENHOE AND STREATLEY AREA

Leave the car park for Sundon Hills with its well arranged picnic area by proceeding away from the road in an easterly direction, with the fenced hedgerow on one's right hand side and the wood-capped spur of Sharpenhoe Clappers clearly seen in the middle distance. Several seats will be found throughout this first part of the walk at strategic viewpoints. In the late spring the fields at the foot of the escarpments shine yellow with oilseed rape in flower.

Continue along the upper hedgeline of this long hilltop sheep-run, then on reaching the corner turn right (south) through the gateway, and **ignore** the green arrows indicating left downhill. On turning a second corner after a few yards on a well defined path, cross the stile. This leads into a narrow meadow which is left by passing through the wide gap in the right hand hedge found about 50 yards from the stile. Enter the field following the boundary round its corner, having just passed the path crossing the field back to Upper Sundon, and look for a footpath sign on a tree which signifies the crossing of the left hand field, still in a generally easterly direction.

On arriving on a trackway turn right uphill for a short way, as if making for the wood on the hilltop. On reaching the nearest corner of the left hand wood use the track alongside the outer perimeter and so complete the last of the triple Z-bends. Enter the tree belt in front of you and immediately bear left onto the path found there, then down the gentle slope, arriving above a wooded combe surrounded by beech trees.

It is worth savouring the atmosphere of this extremely attractive woodland, especially if the sun is filtering through the leafy canopy. Eventually return to the metal footpath signpost. Bear right, using the broad track along the ridge which leaves the tree line after a while to become a well defined track out onto the road. The two Wireless Telegraph masts dominate the skyline of Streatley.

Left at the road for about ½ mile arriving at the Sharpenhoe Clappers car park and undertake this 'leg' of the walk, or continue on the return section saving the Clappers for another excursion. It is in itself an ideal spot for those who have not rambled before.

The Clappers is on the same escarpment as the Sundon Hills. The perambulation around this delightful area pleases all visitors, especially if the map at the car park is read giving information on the natural life hereabouts. Follow the grit road, passing through the gate out onto the path and bearing left at the bend following the hedge (no right turn across the field). This brings one out onto the grassy slopes before the wood. Keep to the lower path, passing a group of stunted fir trees, and enter the Clappers. This wooded spur, or hoo, covered by a cap of boulder clay, has been at one time an Iron Age hill fort, and in mediaeval times a managed rabbit warren controlled by a Warrener.

Beech, the tree of the Chilterns and very tolerant of chalky soils, predominates here, though there is a sprinkling of pine. Follow the perimeter in a clockwise direction providing superb views over 180° of the compass. Invading sycamore trees, alien to these isles until brought over in Roman times, are in the process of being cleared back, though they are rampant on the eastern slopes. There are also patches of the more acceptable ash.

Barton and its hills and cutting can be seen clearly, and also from this high vantage point the now disused lime works alongside the road. The area of Barton Springs is in this direction.

Within the Clappers the tree stumps provide evidence of wood management, and in fact the whole area is now under planned succession control. Help is always needed from volunteers in this immense task, so countryside lovers should give clearance work a thought – Countryside

Rangers can always furnish the addresses of organisers.

Before leaving the trees, look for the memorial obelisk and the touching inscription, as the Clappers is dedicated to the lives of Captain Norman Cairns Robertson of the 2nd Battery of the Hampshire Regiment who died at Hanover in 1917, and of 2nd Lieutenant Lawrence Grant Robertson of the 2nd Battalion Kings Own Scottish Borderers, who met his death on the Somme in 1916.

Make for the incoming path using the upper stretch of the grassy slope and return to the entrance car park through the scrub clearances, down the wooden steps, then on through the copse section.

Right at the road and descend towards Sharpenhoe village, passing disused quarries where chalk was extracted. The much altered Hillview cottage comes into sight, followed by the stucco plastered 'Moleskin' house. This spot provides a fine profile of the Clappers, before turning one's back on them at the footpath sign for the trackway alongside the house. It is a stone surfaced tractor way which skirts the lower side of the wooded scarp slope, yielding extensive views in front.

Eventually the bridleway leaves the slopes and crosses an adjacent field, but the walker continues by the undergrowth on a grass path around a sheep enclosure, which is the floor of this combe. The broad track narrows into a pathway which can have overhanging branches, but do not be deterred. Nettles may also be encountered on this stretch, but the path is clearly there so keep it open by use. The reward is the proximity of the beechwoods on the slopes above. On the other side of this 'box canyon' ignore a footpath sign with a red arrow indicating left up the slope. The way is forward in the broad clear trackway – there are no more difficulties.

Continue around this somewhat circuitous route, passing evidence of hazel coppicing – the age-old method of harvesting wood for wattle, poles, lathes, firwood and many other uses.

To finish the walk, follow the woodland line until a sheep enclosure is reached in a shallow vale. This is crossed down the slope and up the other side, then on arriving at the tree-belt make diagonally left up the next slope to a disused quarry. Here there is a choice. Either use all the yellow arrows down into the pit on a path furnished with a handrail until arriving eventually back at the car, or alternatively, continue over the grassy hilltop to the stile situated in the far left hedgerow corner: then on entering the next field, stay against the fenced hedge on your right hand side and rejoin the outgoing track when it comes into sight. The start point is only a short distance away and in view.

Sheep – the Chilterns Grazers

> **Places included:** LUTON - BARTON IN THE CLAY
>
> **Length of walk:** 7 miles.
>
> **Grid Ref:** Sheet 166 080265
>
> **Parking:** Side road beside St Margaret's Home.
>
> **Bus services:** 76 & 78.
>
> **Public Houses:** Coach and Horses, The Royal Oak, Wagon and Horses (all in Barton).
>
> **Walk Links:** Walk 10 can be reached by leaving Barton in the Clay and walking 1½ miles into Sharpenhoe. Walk 12 is met at Galley Hill on the Icknield Way and further up on the way Walk 13 is reached at Telegraph Hill. (see notes below).
>
> **Notes 1:** Barton Springs are without question the highlight of this walk. In a beautiful setting, it is a delightful spot for children which can be the subject of a short excursion from Barton itself on another occasion.
>
> **2:** The Icknield Way leads through to the Hexton/Hitchin Road, and can be used as a means of making your own walks into Hexton via the Barton Hills or Noon Hill.

SHEEP - THE CHILTERNS GRAZERS

Flocks of sheep once grazed on Dunstable Downs; now in their absence hawthorn scrub has taken a strong hold. Photographs taken at the turn of the century show the clean lines of these hills, and by no means are the Dunstable Downs an isolated case, as the other nearby hills bear witness. Hawthorn scrub pervades chalklands when unchecked.

Dunstable's 13th century merchants exported wool under licence across the Channel. People can still remember sheep in Dunstable which were shepherded down West Street for transport by rail, and no doubt the 'Ewe and Lamb' PH, which stood not far away from the present police station, had some connection.

The Chilterns' chalk downland supported thousands of sheep which were taken back into folds at night. Wherever possible these folds were on arable lands so that the valuable droppings manured the ground. Shepherds living in the wooden huts on iron-wheels of necessity led a lonely life near their flocks.

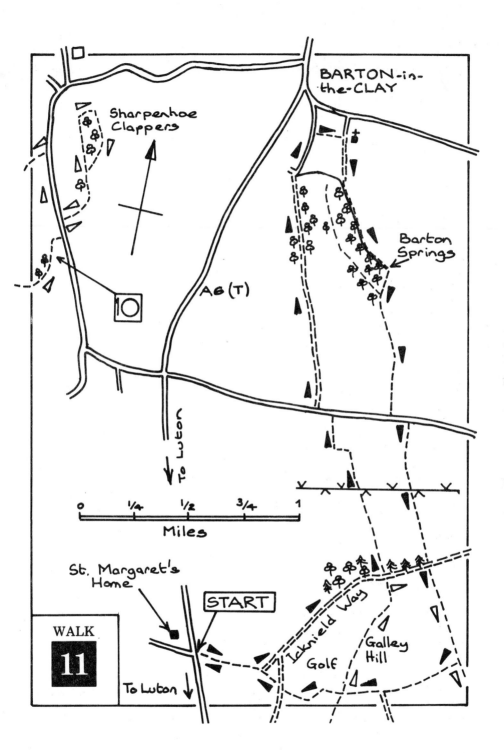

BARTON-in-the-CLAY

Sharpenhoe Clappers

Barton Springs

A6 (T)

To Luton

0   1/4   1/2   3/4   1
Miles

St. Margaret's Home

START

WALK
11

To Luton

Icknield Way

Golf

Galley Hill

Hurdlemaking was an important occupation in these hills for the folds were continually moved. Kale, trefoil, rape and root crops enabled the wintering of the sheep.

But sheep-rearing is not lost, for it continues in the Hockliffe area in fenced fields, whilst on the Pitstone and Barton Hills they have been reintroduced as part of the downland management, reducing scrub and promoting chalk loving flora.

WALK

11

LUTON, BARTON IN THE CLAY

The broad swathe of the Icknield Way is not fully cleared at the outset when you cross the A6 and start alongside the end of the housing. In places the edge of the field will have to be used, but try to use the correct route as much as possible. In fact you can cut back some of the overhanging branches, thereby getting the path fully open. Initially, we are close by modern housing development, and it must be hoped that Luton does not cast its greedy eye on the land on the northern side of the Icknield Way, for the Bramingham area is already lost on the western side.

A bridleway tee junction is met close by the golf course, and here bear sharp left into the broad green way on a definite uphill slope. Galley Hill is very much in evidence and golf fairways are on both sides. Before long, the Maulden fir plantation is reached, and at a crossing of ways we turn left into a broad break across the plantation. Then on the exit side follow the right hand hedge, which may or may not have a path on the headland. The grid lines cross overhead along this section, and then it is up a rise where the boundary dog-legs to the left around a young deciduous tree plantation. Continue northwards on a well defined path out onto the road by a clump of trees.

Hedges hereabouts are very poor stumps with many gaps so it would be a fine gesture if the landowners did some infilling with quicksets, in order to thicken the hedges up. I suppose we should be thankful some still exist in Bedfordshire, but they are not a patch on the Hertfordshire hedges as in the Tea Green/Harpenden area.

So it's a short way left on the road before entering the bridleway which, unfortunately, has a fair amount of rubbish deposited near its entrance. You will find it otherwise unobstructed, making its way between high uncut hedges and offering a pleasant secluded feel of what the old country roads must have been like. Then, after a mile or so, beech woods colonising old chalk quarry workings come into close proximity. Make sure you stay on the broad track as it descends the slope under a canopy of leaves, even though there are several stiles into the woodland. By Hill Farm House we join a road making for Barton then on reaching the playing fields cross them at the signpost towards the church tower, leaving the field between chain-link fencing.

Thatched cottages with 'eyebrow' dormer windows are met at the church, and here is the turning point of the walk. We now make towards Luton on a lane which becomes the very broad bridleway alongside the cemetery. Looking ahead, it appears that we are going into a box-canyon, for the walker can choose either to go upwards beside the woods or take the path beside the stream in the woods, entering just behind the cemetery. The combe gets narrower with trees on all the lower slopes, soon entering the Barton Hills Reserve by means of a tubular gate close by the stream with the woodland path just the other side. The Nature Conservancy Council manage the enclosed grounds, with grazing animals as part of the scrub control scheme. In following the stream up the slope it leads into a spot in a hollow where several springs break the surface into a head-water, and with the canopy of leaf above and the sound of running water, this makes a good spot for a stop.

Cross the headwaters and start ascending the steep slope alongside the boundary fence of Leet Wood which encloses a great variety of trees. You may find it easier to make zig-zag traverses or just take it slowly. On gaining the summit, superb views open out towards Ravensbury hill fort in the woods, and further afield.

Through the stiles at the wood's top corner then left on the bridleway on leaving. Proceed on the enhedged way across the fields, which after awhile becomes a firm track out onto the road near Barton Hill Farm. Head in the direction of the farm a short distance, then take the bridleway in the direction of the Warden Hills. It is extremely good going and in fact the paths on the return are in an even better state than the first part of the walk. Cross over the Icknield Way and you are beside the golf course, so stay on the way which bears slightly left, leaves the course and becomes a field. At the row of mature trees in a substantial hedge stretching right, a well made bridle path is found which takes you out onto an area known as Drays Ditches, with the bridlepath making its way back to Butterfield Green. Continue out onto the Warden and Galley Hills and you will find that the same bridleway makes its route down and across the golf course, meeting on the far side close by the golfhouse. By bearing slightly right and making for the end of the houses, the walker finds himself on the junction of the Icknield Way close by the start. Thread your path back between the hedges.

Walking the Footpaths

Places included: BUTTERFIELD GREEN - WARDEN HILLS

Length of walk: 5½ miles (or 3½ miles).

Start Grid Ref: Sheet 166 105252

Parking: Anywhere from Butterfield Green through to Whitehill Farm, but ensure that no roadway or entrance is obstructed.

Bus services: 92, 94, 95, 96, 97, 98 and 99.

Public Houses: Public houses in Stopsley, Luton.

Walk Links: The start of Walk 13 is passed in Lilley. See also walk link notes for Walk 11.

Notes 1: See note 2 with Walk 11.

2: The 3½ mile option on very even tracks makes it ideal for children just starting rambling and for those wanting an easy stroll.

WALKING THE FOOTPATHS

A survey by the Countryside Commission in 1986 revealed that only 12% of the public walking in the countryside used non-signposted paths, since it involved mapreading. A further 22% walked on signposted paths and 25% stayed on open spaces, commons and beaches; the rest stayed on country roads.

The 120,000 miles of rights-of-way provide a most important access into the countryside, much of which is under threat from barbed-wire, minimal maintenance, ploughed-out paths (especially alongside grubbed out hedgerows) and obstructions of all sorts including new building work. Admittedly numbers of them have diversions, particularly through new housing estates or because of new road systems. Usage of our remaining footpath system is of utmost importance for its survival.

This country now has 13 long distance routes totalling 1676 miles, and a further 300 other routes identified and promoted by individuals, Councils and organisations. As a spin-off countryside access has increased, with the public venturing out onto other pathways.

If it was not for the members of the Ramblers' Association doing the footpath clearances in the winter months, most of our footpaths would be lost by

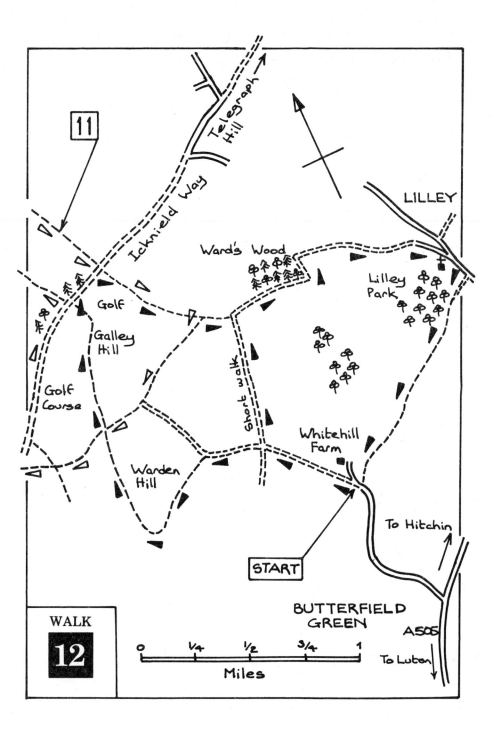

11

Telegraph Hill

Icknield Way

LILLEY

Ward's Wood

Lilley Park

Golf

Galley Hill

Golf Course

Short walk

Whitehill Farm

Warden Hill

START

To Hitchin

BUTTERFIELD GREEN

A505

To Luton

WALK

12

0   ¼   ½   ¾   1
Miles

now. Unless overhanging boughs were cut and nettles and brambles cleared, these obstructions would act as a deterrent in the summer months. Conservation Corps, Open Space societies, Parish councils and increasingly youth schemes are playing their part, awareness and action being of considerable importance. Matters can enter the legal world if landowners seek extinguishments and diversions.

WALK
12

BUTTERFIELD GREEN - WARDEN HILLS

This walk can be shortened at will, with the variants mentioned as they arise.

Commence down the broad way beside the trim farm drive offering high views out over Luton (it can be very cold and windswept up here at times) until the Icknield Way is met. The going is excellent on well made tracks. On reaching a crossways of lanes, by choosing the right hand lane the short version is taken (alternative 1, see map). But otherwise continue in the direction of the hills in front – the stunted, distorted trees provide a testimony to the windstrengths. On the slight bend right of the main way take the left hand path following the hedgerow and descending the slopes of the hill. Make sure you keep on the right of the hedge and tree line. In skirting the big hill-top field the crest of Warden Hill is traversed, meeting up with the path given in alternative 2, (see also below).

Along the summit above the scrub belt which borders the golf course, noting that the ridges form part of what is known as Dray's Ditches, with the road to Bedford clearly seen. On arriving at the end of the ridge line we are now on Galley Hill; Sharpenhoe Clappers, a wooded spur in the N.N.W. is visible, and Barton Springs and Telegraph Hill are not far away, as featured in walks 12 and 13. Leave the summit in a northward direction, then with care pass over the golf fairway by a well defined route which leads into the green lane of the Icknield Way. We are now by a wood with a lane crossing a little way up on your right, (as included in the Barton Springs walk) but stay on the Icknield Way up to the main lane crossing. Sharp right here along the broad bridleway bounding the golf course.

Now onward staying on the bridleway which leaves the golf course, bearing slightly left into the beginning of a green lane. At the first hedge and treeline is a substantial track turning off on the right, which is alternative 2, and by following it round, the left hand bend takes the walker back to Whitehill Farm on the outgoing route. (A link onto Galley Hill can be used if making your own variations – see map).

After a short distance the return of alternative 1 is met. The green way follows the perimeter of the conifer plantation, Ward's Wood, which turns rightward leaving the plantation, still on the trackway, crossing open ground into a pair of hedgerows. And so to Box End cottage with its pronounced English bond brickwork, and continue into Lilley, a village of interest, particularly its church.

On the through road continue ahead past the church, looking out for the Cassel Memorial Hall, at which point cross the road and take the track in front of the Hall leading from the car-park.

This lane can be muddy at times, passing playing fields on your left, and then on beside Illey Park, which is a woodland estate, the track becoming a grassy path as it enters the Park. Carry on past the wood in a straight line across a field and through the gap in the hedge, then up the slope in front beside a solitary tree.

On the brow three white or colour painted stiles can be seen in a straight line slightly leftward crossing small fields. There are no difficulties, and the road is rejoined at the commencement.

Highways of Antiquity

Places included: LILLEY - TELEGRAPH HILL - WELLBURY - LITTLE OFFLEY

Length of walk: 6½ miles.

Grid Ref: Sheet 166 118266

Parking: Discreet parking in the village near the start.

Bus services: 92, 94, 95, 96, 97, 98 and 99.

Public Houses: The Silver Lion (Lilley), The Lilley Arms (Lilley), The Fox (Pirton).

Walk Links: The start of this walk is on the circuit of Walk 12. Walk 14 can be reached by the byroad from Little Offley to Gt Offley or the bridleway from Lilley Hoo to Westbury Wood.

Notes 1: As has been said in Walk 11, the Icknield Way can be used for other walks of your own, and on this particular walk Pirton can be reached on the bridleway skirting Tingley Wood.

2: Telegraph Hill need not be scaled on the walk, but the views are worthwhile, being recognised as such by the Ordnance Survey. Also, the southern end of Lilley Hoo is a good viewing point.

HIGHWAYS OF ANTIQUITY

Commencing in the Hunstanton area in Norfolk and passing on through Thetford not far from Grimes Graves, the Icknield Way continues into Bedfordshire, follows the Chiltern Escarpment, then crosses the River Thames near Goring, finishing at Wansborough in Wiltshire near Avebury. Naturally, both ends had feeder trackways and other ancient ways across the Way, which is not all clearly defined in present times. Why this neolithic 'highway' came about still remains a matter for deliberation by historians, but it was in existence long before Londinium became a Roman port and an important crossing point of the Thames for several highways.

Southwestwards from Ivinghoe Beacon the Way has taken on the name Ridgeway, inaugurated in 1973 with an acorn as a symbol on the waymarking, a total of 85 miles in length. A number of useful guidebooks describe this Long Distance path. (The Berkshire Downs Ridgeway is considered older than the Icknield Way).

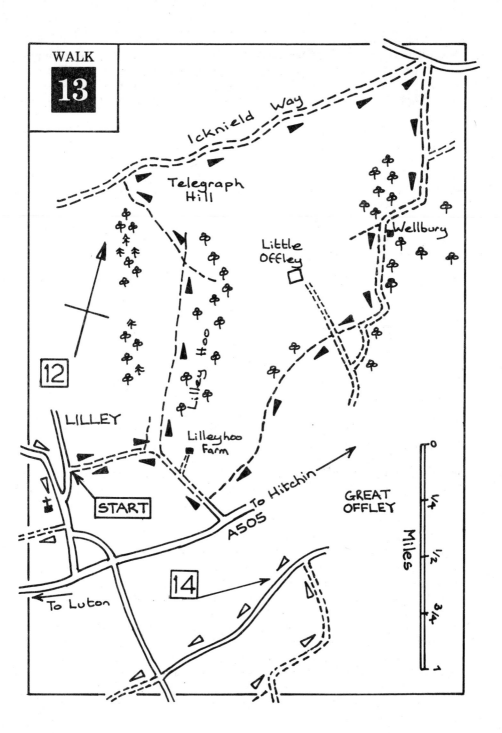

WALK

13

Icknield Way

Telegraph Hill

Little Offley

Wellbury

Lilley Hoo

LILLEY

Lilleyhoo Farm

START

To Hitchin

A505

GREAT OFFLEY

To Luton

12

14

Miles

0

1/4

1/2

3/4

1

Within the area covered by walks in this book maps show the Icknield Way as a single track, whereas from Wendover southwards, Upper and Lower Ways are shown and there may have been other alternatives. For the Icknield Way was an 'all weather' route over the centuries, with the Lower Way following the approximate water line of springs whilst the Upper Way stayed on the drier hilltops.

From Ivinghoe Beacon to the M1 motorway the A505 has adopted the Icknield Way, but the original route went through Leagrave, crossing the present A6 and surviving these days as the green way going by Telegraph Hill and on towards Hitchin. In the early 19th century a semaphore signalling tower stood on the hill transmitting the Trafalgar and Waterloo messages northwards – hence its name.

In Dunstable another trackway from Dunstable Downs continues as Half Moon Lane and follows the foot of Blows Downs; in fact it is a parallel course for the Icknield Way at a higher level.

WALK

13

LILLEY, TELEGRAPH HILL, WELLBURY, LITTLE OFFLEY

The signposted bridleway is at the right of house No. 20 at the end of the terrace, having a good surface and descending between high hedges into a shallow vale. Pass over the crossing of the ways, rising up the broad green slope into the trees ahead, where it is worth stopping for a moment to enjoy the views, especially over the village, though they will be encountered again on the return.

Through the belt of trees bear left at the wooden Telegraph Hill sign and stay against the high hedge at this end of the very long field. Arrive at a tee junction with a green way coming up from the A505, one of the vista points of the walk looking southward. Turn north (ie. left) on the tractor track/bridleway staying on it right across this large field about a mile in length, and although other paths cross the way ignore them. From the map it can be seen that this is the area known as Lilley Hoo, having woods and clumps of trees close at hand, one of the joys of the walk.

Onwards towards the twin overhead power grid system with the eastern flanks of the Warden and Galley Hills seen in the middle distance. The Ordnance Survey map shows the recognised viewing places in a blue symbol.

The way now has some bends and a bridleway into the nearby woods is encountered, not part of the route; then about 100 yards on is a clearly placed bridleway sign at a crossing. Follow the direction of the blue arrow, indicating a path which proceeds diagonally left across an arable field towards a copse on the skyline. (Disregard the sharp left track alongside an oak tree and accompanying hedge). On reaching the brow it is found that the bridleway descends through trees to join the Icknield Way, offering clear views of the wooded Barton Hills, the subject of Walks 10 & 11. Just before reaching the tree-lined Icknield Way proper, an easy broad grassy slope is found on the right hand side – leading up to the summit – this is Telegraph Hill.

This noted scenic spot offers views over the two Streatley Wireless Telegraphy masts, with the inverted triangular shape of the Sundon water tower on out past Dunstable Downs, culminating in Ivinghoe Beacon and the misty outlines beyond. Then northwards lie the Clophill/Maulden Woods, with the Bedford area on the distant skyline. Beech, birch, ash, hazel and blackthorn grow hereabouts, together with other species; for a lover of the arboreal the whole walk is a pleasure.

Continue over the brow of the hill into the broad stretch of the Icknield Way, tree and hedge lined in this part, which enters after a while the more open terrain of the Hitchin area beyond the tree-capped hills northeastward. Hedgerows with their spaced trees criss-cross the area, their retention deserving a special tribute for those who farm these Beds/Herts borders, unlike their brethren in mid-Beds who have swept so many of these natural corridors aside by mass grubbing-out. On down the slope past the pronounced form of Deacon Hill on the other side of the left hand hedgerow and join the B655 Hitchin road. A couple of hundred yards up the road a bridleway is met with the left side leading up past Tingley Wood to Pirton, but our way is right at the sign stating 2 miles for Gt Offley.

The thatched Wellbury cottage is met, built as a single storey on a cross ground plan, having moulded dripstone hoods above windows which are of the casement type. Unlike Suffolk and the West Country which are still literally littered with thatched cottages of every description, there is only a sprinkling of these English gems here in the northern Chilterns. Continuing along the bridleway Wellbury comes into view, a large white residence displaying fretted bargeboards at the many gables.

Continue up the road past the tall mature chestnut trees on your left sprinkled with young spruce, and on reaching the fine oak on the bend of the road, look through the hedgerow gap and see the tower blocks of Stevenage clearly visible in the middle disance. On reaching the unmistakeable South Lodge with its finialed bargeboards on the bend of the driveway, leave the driveway and proceed on the right hand side of a broad bridleway in a southwest direction.

Head towards the twin sets of overhead grid lines encountered on the outward stretches. After 200 yards or so pass over the bridleway crossing and Little Offley Manor is seen up the right hand slope. It is of Tudor origin built in H-plan, and when given a facade renovation a central pediment was incorporated together with sash windows, all set in a strong red brickwork.

Ahead of us is a gentle downward slope towards the rather distracting A505 whose traffic sounds, plus the occasional roar of aircraft noise from Luton Airport, jars the tranquility of the area. Prominent on the left hand skyline Gt Offley's telecommunication tower stands supporting its microwave aerial dishes whilst triple power cables on regular poles accompany the walker.

Keep going forward towards the road ignoring the track-turning to the right, and accompany the left hand hedgerow joining the minor road close by the Hitchin road.

Turn right upwards on the road into a grassy slope, passing the red-bricked farm and ascending to the gentle summit. For confirmation a wooden sign for Telegraph Hill is noticed near the top and the outgoing signpost comes into view through a gap in the hedges. This is one of the recognised viewing points of the walk in a southerly direction.

Bear left and retrace the first section of the walk which affords fine elevations in the Luton direction.

Chalk Hills Natural History

Places included: LUTON - OUTSKIRTS OF GT. OFFLEY - PUTTERIDGEBURY

Length of walk: 5 miles.

Start Grid Ref: Sheet 166 115242.

Parking: Putteridgebury Leisure Centre car-park at the end of Putteridge Road, Stopsley.

Bus services: 92, 94, 95, 96, 97, 98 and 99.
Alight at the Stopsley roundabout.

Public Houses: King William IV (Mangrove Green), The Bull (Gt. Offley), The Green Man (Gt. Offley), The Red Lion (Gt. Offley).

Walk Links: Walk 13 can be reached on the road between Gt. Offley and Little Offley or the bridleway out to Lilley Hoo.

Notes 1: A network of minor roads and bridleways encompass Mangrove Green, Cockernhoe, Wanden End, Tea Green, Breachwood Green and Diamond End, and with Luton expanding this end of the Airport, a totally satisfactory walk cannot be devised. However the high ground around here provides a good vantage point for Luton Airport activity.

2: The area bounded by King's Walden, Preston, St. Paul's Walden and Whitwell provides countryside for making your own walks in the knowledge that the Queen Mother spent some of her childhood here!

CHALK HILLS NATURAL HISTORY

The Bedfordshire Natural History Society's new book entitled "Bedfordshire Wildlife" comes at an opportune time, filling a noticeable gap in the County's literature. It not only reviews the distribution of flora but has a comprehensive coverage of mammals, molluscs and insects.

'The Chalk Downs' is considered a major region in Bedfordshire from a natural history standpoint. These hills support at least nine varieties of British orchids along with cowslips, harebells, bluebells, the Chiltern Gentian,

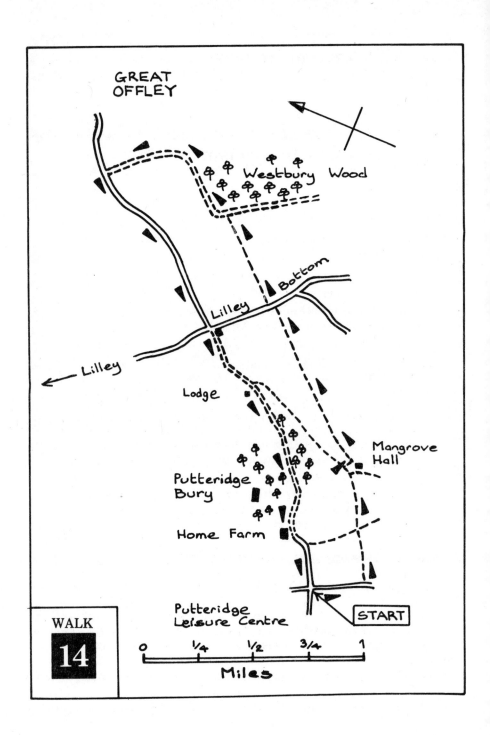

GREAT
OFFLEY

Westbury Wood

Bottom

Lilley

Lilley

Lodge

Putteridge
Bury

Mangrove
Hall

Home Farm

Putteridge
Leisure Centre

START

WALK
14

0   ¼   ½   ¾   1

Miles

70

primroses, pasque-flowers and trefoils. Dunstable Downs were famed for skylarks, netted and eaten in lark-pie; they are now only thirteenth in the list of breeding birds here, quite likely as a result of the loss of open grasslands. Willow warblers are well in the clear at the top of the breeding list, followed by yellowhammers, dunnocks, robins and blackbirds.

The use of natural history books and guides will enable the visitor to recognise the varied wildlife on these hills, which are managed by the Countryside Commission as Sites of Special Scientific Interest.

LUTON - OUTSKIRTS OF GT. OFFLEY - PUTTERIDGEBURY **14**

Commencement is down Selsey Drive away from the Leisure Centre following the wall of the Bury, and where the Drive makes an abrupt stop the Mangrove Green sign indicates the way beside a playing field. Continue along this wall, which is rather sorry for itself in places having patched holes, then cross the access driveway coming from Mangrove Green. Cross the stile ahead and go up to the place where there is a large gap in the fence connecting with a paddock/ orchard at the rear of a farm which is built in a 'double-pile' form having an 'M' shaped end roofline and barge-board decorated dormer windows. (There are quite a number of double-pile buildings in Dunstable – Chews School being the best example). Make your way to the rear of the farm.

Walk across to the gate in the corner and go through, making sure it is closed, then turn sharp left onto a grassy track leading directly away from the rear of the farm. One of several tree-planting schemes on the walk is passed, so look out from here for the views along the vale of Lilley Bottom – they are fine so don't hurry. The flyover seen on the far left is the link for the Lilley on the Great Offley bypass. Scattered about are clumps of mixed woodland in addition to tree belts, one of the pleasures of this walk. Stay on the well surfaced track – you can do no other – and descend into the bottom, arriving beside a house with white dormer windows called "Baronsfield". Once on the road look for the footpath sign indicating Westbury in front of the house.

It directs toward a 'notch' in the wood on the skyline, but in getting there the path crosses the big field in front of you. Dependent upon the crops the path may change direction on the up, and meets a country lane running in front, so make your way towards the gap.

The lane goes through this notch on the boundary of Westbury Wood and down into a depression – fairly shallow – then up the other side arriving right in a corner. Now pass anticlockwise round and stay in this field ignoring the right hand path for Great offley. It is a broad green way and, keeping the hedge at your right hand side, come out onto the road beside a bungalow. Left here on this very rural road connecting Offley with Putteridge, a lovely road with good mixed scenery whose trees are not indiscriminately ripped out – and it's downhill!

On meeting the junction with the Lilley Bottom road cross over, then walk

71

by the Lodge Cottage with its fretted bargeboard gables. On the very good stony track between uncut hedges gently go up a gradient passing the East Lodge bungalow on the drive. Here a path for Mangrove Green shoots off on the outside of the boundary wall which can be used as a variation of this walk another time. We enter a parkland estate heavily wooded in places gaining glimpses of Putteridge House nearing the top of the rise away on our right.

And so on in front of the farm built on a 'model' farm basis, with a wagon shed at the rear and the outbuildings around the stock-yards having round-headed windows. The farmhouse beside the farm sports finials on the much-fretted gables bargeboards. A somewhat strange looking octagonal building with narrow hooded slit windows is discovered. Then the walk concludes by using the drive through the tree belt within the boundary wall.

Someres Scene

Places included: SOMERIES - CHILTERN GREEN

Length of walk: 3 miles.

Grid Ref: Sheet 166 125200

Parking: Vicinity of Copt Hall, ensuring no obstructions are caused. Copt Hall can be reached as a turning off the A 6129 Luton/ Wheathampstead road.

Bus services: 44.

Public Houses: The Bright Star (Peter's Green).

Walk Links: The start of Walk 16 is close at hand on Chiltern Green, and the start of the Lea Valley Walk (17) is at the Copt Hall road turning.

Notes 1: Another simple walk suitable for children on several counts and with a wood belt on the return, safe for playing and hiding in, but the interest element comes with looking through the perimeter fence of Luton Airport, while the Someries Gatehouse, and the ruined foundations of Someries Castle behind, should really exercise their imaginations.

SOMERIES SCENE

The gatehouse and chapel are all that survive at Someries, but it is important by virtue of being one of the earliest brick buildings in Bedfordshire. Commencement of the building work is thought to date from 1448; the making and usage of brickwork as exemplified at Someries is very advanced bearing in mind that the art of brickmaking was lost soon after the departure of the Romans from these shores.

The blind cusping and arcading together with the corbelling is quite a considerable feat for its age. The door and window heads also are similarly impressive in a building nearly 550 years old. Driphoods that shed rainwater from around windows are here in carved brick, a feature that has its origins in stone-masonry. This gem is now in the care of the Department of the Environment who have put this structure in good order.

Someries Castle proper only has foundations for view and is situated behind the gatehouse.

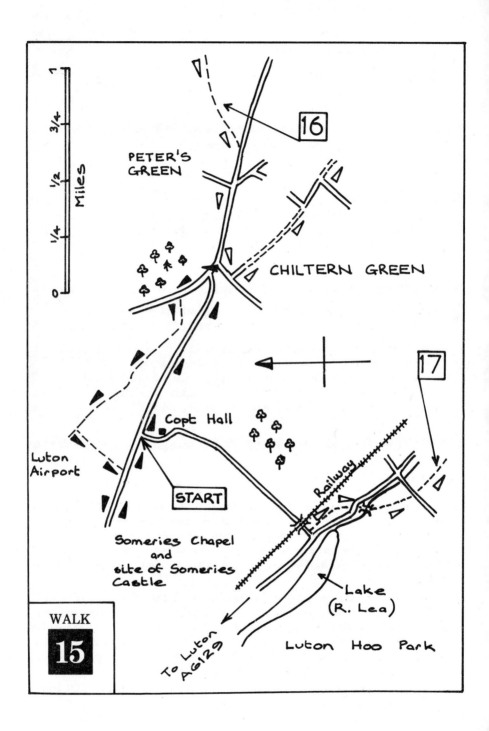

PETER'S GREEN

16

CHILTERN GREEN

17

Miles
1
3/4
1/2
1/4
0

Copt Hall

START

Luton
Airport

Railway

Someries Chapel
and
site of Someries
Castle

Lake
(R. Lea)

Luton Hoo Park

To Luton
A6129

WALK
15

SOMERIES, CHILTERN GREEN

The first part of this walk leads away from Luton Airport, with a scattering of trees along the roadside. There won't be many cars here and birds can usually be heard singing. We are making for a broad belt of trees and the road bends as it goes through; we then find ourselves on a diminutive green which may be considered an outlier for Chiltern Green proper. In front of the timber-framed house turn left up the Tea Green road passing Forge Cottage. Now look carefully for the Bridleway sign just a few yards further up on the other side of the road. The sign indicates a broad hedge and a footpath which is cleared by local groups from time to time.

After a short distance the path is found on a hedgebank, then it does a dog-leg turn into a wide swathe of trees which acts as a bird shelter in winter-time. This fine treebelt takes you up to the perimeter fence of Luton Airport close by a red rotating radar scanner and provides a clear sight of the airport buildings and aircraft activity.

The way out is along an old hedgeline marked now by a row of scattered trees – better these than nothing at all, though a hedge would provide better screening.

This brings us back onto the road, which has not really left our company for most of the walk. So before rendezvous-ing with your vehicles take a walk and see Someries Castle beside the farm. The building seen is a Tudor gatehouse and chapel under the protection of the Ministry, and behind are the foundations of the castle itself built from 1448. The Wenlock family, builders of Someries, have a chapel named after them in Luton parish church.

Make sure you look out in the direction of Luton Hoo when returning. The woods hereabouts were planted deliberately by past owners of Luton Hoo for wooded horizon vistas seen from their home.

Bricks and Mortar

Places included: CHILTERN GREEN - LITTLE CUTTS - ANSELLS END - PETER'S GREEN

Length of walk: 5 miles.

Start Grid Ref: Sheet 166 135194

Parking: Discreet parking on the edge of the green.

Bus services: 44.

Public Houses: The Bright Star (Peter's Green).

Walk Links: Walk 15 is encountered and it is perfectly possible to combine the two together. The start of Walk 17 is at the Copt Hall road turning and can be used for a new walk outlined in the notes below.

Notes 1: This is a neat enjoyable walk using several bridleways in an area that has many of its hedges surviving and with very few people about; the roadside signposts act as a check.

2: Hertfordshire seems a far better county at safeguarding its hedges, trees and woodlands, as this walk will confirm.

3: A full circular walk is suggested, using Walk 17 down to Cold Harbour in Batford and taking the B652 Kimpton Road, then joining this walk at Dane Farm and returning via Copt Hall.

BRICKS AND MORTAR

The 16th and 17th centuries saw the period known as the Great Rebuilding, particularly in rural areas when decaying houses were demolished and village expansion accelerated.

With this period came land cultivation improvements with farmhouses built out in the middle of their lands, a departure from the farmhouse being situated on the village street. Another concurrent rural development comes with the origins of village 'ends', some having manufacturing connections.

Fewer new great houses were created (though many were substantially improved or rebuilt) and certainly no castles built; vernacular building of all sizes went on apace.

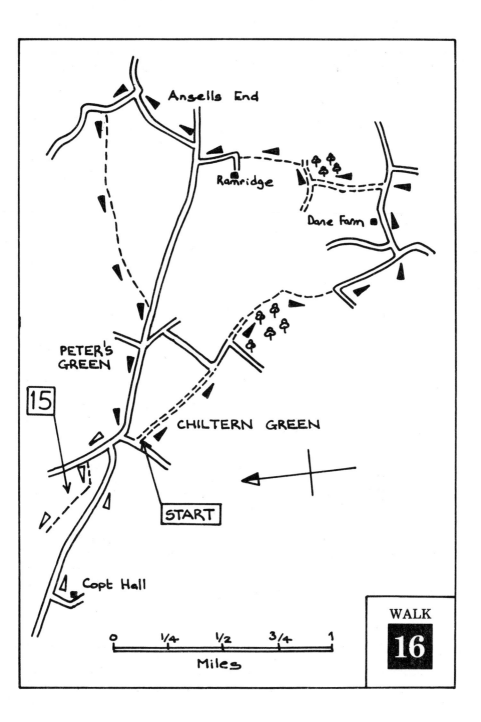

Ansells End

Ramridge

Dane Farm

PETER'S
GREEN

15

CHILTERN GREEN

START

Copt Hall

WALK
16

0   1/4   1/2   3/4   1

Miles

Buildings of the Chilterns fall within the country's brick walling materials zone, with knapped flint as an alternative taking over from the timber-framing tradition which in this region had vertical studding infilled with wattle and daub; then later brick noggin was used.

Thatch roofing in either straw or reed was the norm, followed in later centuries by plain tiling (non-corrugated) for slates don't appear until the latter half of the 19th century, carried by the new railways. The most enduring of all village buildings, the village church, reflected local fortunes or otherwise, often the sole survivor of a settlement. Only stone could really do for a church, though there are exceptions. Totternhoe stone never had a blameless reputation as a result of its bad weathering properties.

CHILTERN GREEN - LITTLE CUTTS - ANSELLS END - PETER'S GREEN

Start by the timber-framed Laburnham Farm, with its attractive series of gables, at the bottom corner of the Green.

Here the outgoing track will be found, with a good stony surface alongside cottages and houses, leading out as a partially sunken lane in the field. The bridleway joins a road for a short stretch, then, when the road bears right sharply, we go straight on the track ahead beside a large expanse of woodland. This section is often very muddy so be warned, and as we progress the track narrows into footpath width, but it is maintained and bounded in places by a cut hedge. The important thing is that you must stay on this path on leaving the road, which has several twists and turns and side paths. After a while we begin to lose height, and the hedges with their occasional trees make pleasant surrounds. Cut back any overhanging branches in these sections.

The path joins an access road by a bend along by a flint cottage, and this road brings you out on the B652 road connecting Kimpton with Harpenden. Go sharp left up the rise and ignore the first side turn. Up on the nearby hill is a tree-lined hollow which makes one wonder if it was man-made and worked for flint. Pass the feather-boarded Dane Farm whose old cross aisle doorway for the threshing floor is unmistakeable. Look out for the unusual corner-wise-built chimney stacks on the farm. Then not far on is the bridleway sign, a wooden gate and several stumps for horse passage. Enter the bridleway, which is almost a lane, lined with great hedges and trees bringing you alongside a large wood on your right. At the top end turn clockwise round the wood (R) *not* straight on. This bordering lane after a short while breaks out from the wood's edge facing a large field.

In the middle distance can be seen another wood which may or may not have a track heading for the right hand edge which is our next stage, (whether there are crops or not the bridleway is on the map.) Your direction is north, and as you pass the wood on your left stay with the hedgerow past a field of agricultural equipment and sheds, making for a haybarn. There is a short greenway gap alongside the pair of farmworkers' houses, and join up with the Ramridge Farm access road, which has tree planting in the hedgerow gaps, coming out on the through road by a bridleway sign. Turn right in the direction of Kimpton and after a little distance left at the sign post for Ansells End. Hereabouts there are extensive views over arable lands still with plentiful trees and woods, such an important feature of the countryside. On past Russells Farm with its cambered arch window lintels and dentilated gable ends, then down a slope to a pair of adjoining farms on a small green, certainly worth more than a second look if you are interested in vernacular architecture.

We leave on the narrow Wanden Green road which is signposted on this rising, turning country road. Holly can be found on either side of these hedgelined embanked sides, planted by country folk in times past so that the lanes could be distinguished when snow lay heavy. Watch out, as you make the first descent, for the Peters Green bridleway sign tucked up under trees on the left hand bank on the approach to a bend. Enter this long narrow field by the gate on the bend, remembering to close it, and walk along staying by the southern boundary, and at the far end is a gate for horse-riders.

Now comes a decision, for the hedgerow before you may have a used footpath on either side and the choice is yours, though you may find that it peters out on one side or another, so just pass through the several gaps found. In the end you must have the hedge on your left hand side in the field which is slightly lower than its neighbour. The way is now continuous, keeping the bank always on your left, and comes out onto a road by a Baptist chapel on your left and mature aged houses on your other hand, many being refurbished. The sign for Ansells End confirms we are correct.

What appears to be a chapel converted into domestic use can be noticed, recognisable by its apse on the eastern end, and we come to the "Bright Star" public house on Peters Green itself. Staying on the road we complete the walk on to Chiltern Green.

The Upper Lea Valley

Places included: LUTON - EAST HYDE - BATFORD - HARPENDEN

Length of walk: 4½ miles.

Grid Ref: Sheet 166 118188

Parking: Copt Hall road turning on the A 6129 Luton/Wheathampstead road, close by the start.

Bus services: Nil.

Public Houses: The Leather Bottle (East Hyde), Gibralter Castle (Batford), Red Cow (Harpenden), The Marquis of Granby (Harpenden).

Walk Links: See Walk Links for Walk 16.

Notes 1: This is a linear walk, hence the bus and train information.

2: A circular walk can be made by taking the B652 Kimpton road at Batford, joining Walk 16 at Dane Farm and returning via Copt Hall.

3: In effect the Lea Valley walk in its entirety is South Bedfordshire's Long Distance Footpath, having its start in Leagrave Marsh, close by Wauluds Bank earthworks. A concerted wildlife conservation clean-up effort is underway, so let's hope that all the authorities and landowners make the LVLDF a success. It has the bonus of riverain interests.

4: Harpenden can be used for touring and walking, sweeping from Hemel Hempstead, the northern outskirts of St Albans, Brocket Hall Park, Wheathampstead and the Ayots in the east.

THE UPPER LEA VALLEY

South Bedfordshire's only river of any consequence, the River Lea, rises in Leagrave at the northern end of Luton, fringes Harpenden, Wheathampstead and Welwyn, passes through Hertford and Ware, then south into Enfield, Haringey and Hackney, before joining the Thames in Dockland.

Many parts along its length can be walked but more access agreements need

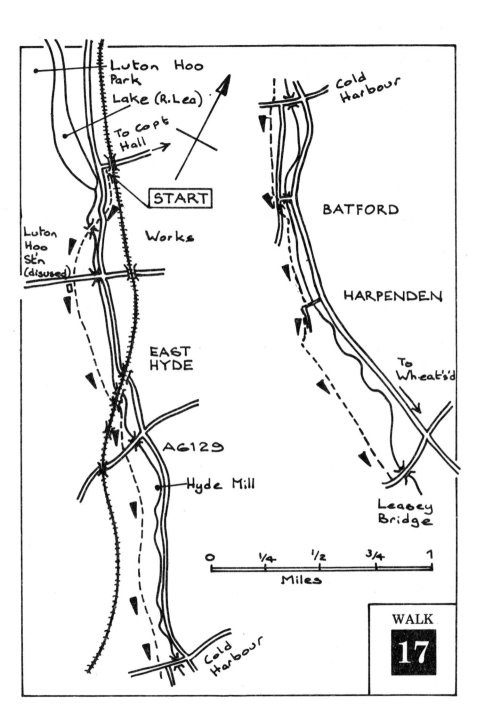

Luton Hoo
Park
Lake (R.Lea)

To Copt
Hall

START

Luton
Hoo
St'n
(disused)

Works

EAST
HYDE

AG129

Hyde Mill

Cold
Harbour

Cold
Harbour

BATFORD

HARPENDEN

To
Wheat's'd

Leasey
Bridge

0   1/4   1/2   3/4   1
Miles

WALK
17

securing. The stretch from the outskirts of Luton to the edge of Harpenden is designated, but the full approval of the landowners has not yet been secured.

For the most part, the bed of the former Hatfield, Luton and Dunstable Railway is the route of the Upper Lea Valley walk, though the earlier clearance work is now growing over. However, assuming official sanction Luton will eventually be on one of the country's long distance footpaths. In the meantime, follow the way described and users can be making a contribution towards its opening.

LUTON, EAST HYDE, BATFORD, HARPENDEN

Between the road and the railway bridge enter the tree plantation on the right over a stile bearing the Lea Valley swan symbol, then follow a narrow path through the saplings, such as it is, rising within 100 yards onto the bed of the tree-lined old railway track. Continue along the line and possibly through patches of nettles, until the embankment comes to an abrupt end where the rail bridge abutments should be. Descend the bank and cross over the fence at the bend in the road. This is a very busy road, so be very careful when crossing, and make for the gap in the hedge on the opposite side. Within yards is a stile on the right hand side; cross and back towards the road just crossed and the path up the embankment is discovered at the road's end, taking you up onto the railway track level again. Follow the line which crosses the River Lea by a concrete bridge going behind the Hyde sewerage works, but make sure that you stay between the two fences as the track goes through the tree belt, for it is somewhat overgrown in this area and the path wanders.

Cross the road and over the far stile at the derelict Luton Hoo station and keep on the railbed through the low cutting in front past the buildings. More of the works is found on your left but keep a look-out for log steps set in the bank on your right. Up the steps, making a point of staying outside the barbed wire fence on the right and the link fence on the left, then after a while the beech tree belt can be used if the path is too overgrown. Soon, the mainline railway for St Pancras draws nearer so at the viaduct rejoin the old railbed, passing under the arches, then it is found that we are now at the top edge of a small field that leads out onto a rural road.

Now cross yonder fence, returning back on the alignment of the rail route. At once it is noticeable that conservation and management work has made the sections quite scenic with glades and open spaces on the way, and scatterings of young trees. The mill at East Hyde comes into view with the river leaving the millpond by two weirs; now we follow the hedgeline through the open fields, while close by flows the river amongst tree plantations.

Cross the fences at the ends of the fields, returning again onto the rail bed and thence into a wooded cutting, which after several hundred yards takes us up another set of log steps close by the Red Cow PH. Straight over the road, taking the path between the houses, on the rail bed again along the tree-lined embankment, then follow the path down onto the road. The Upper Lea Valley path passes round a modern church, then through an area of allotments, open spaces and playing fields, bringing the walker close by Batford Mill in an area that's been the subject of a lot of conservation work near the Gibralter Castle PH. On reaching the ford and bridge of Crabtree Lane turn right and go up to the Marquis of Granby PH. Left here, and after a short distance, bear right onto our old friend the railway track. Again through a wooded zone crossing the rail bridge, we now have possibly the most scenic part of this walk, for being higher than the river the views look across the meanders and trees. On the far side of the river disused cressbeds can be seen. And so the end comes into sight at the road crossing Leasey bridge.

Brickmaking

Places included: CADDINGTON - WOODSIDE - MARKYATE - ALEY GREEN

Length of walk: 6½ miles.

Grid Ref: Sheet 166 064198

Parking: Around the perimeter of Caddington Green.

Bus services: 230, 231 and 232.

Public Houses: The Cricketers (Caddington), The Harrow (Woodside).

Walk Links: Caddington Green is the turning point of Walk 19. See Note 1 below.

Notes 1: Luton Hoo Park, A6 (T) road to Harpenden and the M1 motorway all prevent satisfactory links with the previous group of walks.

   2: Since most people never see the High Street in Markyate, as the village is bypassed, this walk provides an opportunity for a closer look at a village distinguished especially by its vernacular buildings.

   3: Markyate is a good launching place for exploring Flamstead through to Redbourn and the northern outskirts of Hemel Hempstead.

BRICKMAKING

Until well into the twentieth century brickmaking was a flourishing industry in and around Caddington, with fifteen recorded brickyards. Clay would be dug out of pits on the hilltops in the autumn or early winter, then stacked so that frosts broke it down. In springtime began the 12-hour-day of puddling the clay into a cake-mix consistency by wetting and stirring in 'pugmills', usually powered by a horse walking round and round, working a 'gin'.

   The paste-like mixture would either be beaten into shaped brick moulds or extruded and wire-cut, then in this 'green' state air-dried for a month or more under cover in readiness for later firing – in early days in a clamp, but in more recent times always in a kiln. Millions of bricks were made on a contract basis, usually by very small enterprises. All stages of the work involved exceptional labouring in digging, windlasses, millworking, shovelling the clay in and digging

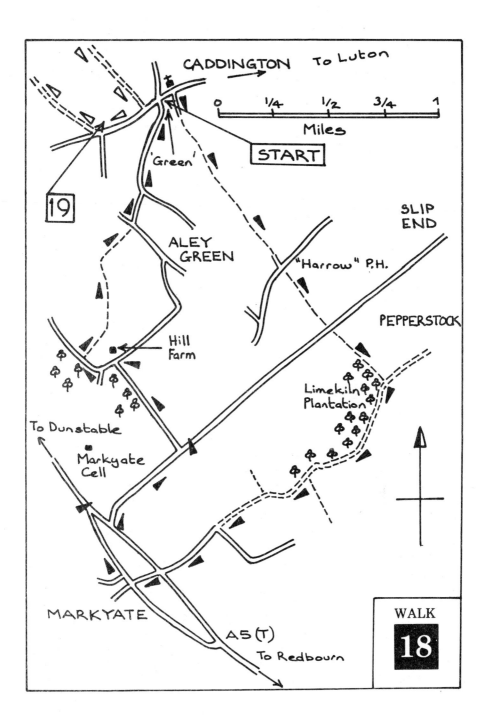

CADDINGTON To Luton

0   ¼   ½   ¾   1

Miles

START

SLIP END

'Green'

ALEY GREEN

"Harrow" P.H.

PEPPERSTOCK

19

Hill Farm

Limekiln Plantation

To Dunstable

Markyate Cell

MARKYATE

A5 (T)

To Redbourn

WALK
18

85

it out, watering etc., as well as all the manual stages in making and moving the bricks themselves.

Clays in the Luton, Caddington and Kensworth areas contained a certain amount of iron oxide, producing a grey, plum or purplish brick, whilst the gault clays towards Cambridgeshire contain lime, producing a yellow brick. Quite a number of buildings can be found with the yellowish brick, but the 'Luton' brick predominates in the towns before the great building expansions from the late 1940s onwards. South Bedfordshire has no brickmaking these days, though the sites in the Caddington area are still distinguishable.

Found on the hilltops in South Bedfordshire are the beds of clay-with-flints used in the old brickyards; further north stretch the gault clays also used for brickmaking, then comes the Greensand ridge; beyond lie the Oxford clays, a stiff blue material, the basis for Bedfordshire's brick industry. Also boulder clays can be found as pockets deposited from the Ice Ages.

Brickmaking consumed vast acres of woodland for kiln fuel until the coming of coals and cokes, so coppicing proved a valuable source of wood. In coppicing, young growth from the 'bole' or 'stool' of a cut-down tree is cropped commercially for the supply of poles, hurdles, handles, faggots, and of course, kiln fuel. Charcoal burners needed great supplies for their clamps, particularly the early iron-smelters of Surrey for their 'hammers', ie. forges.

WALK

CADDINGTON, WOODSIDE, MARKYATE, ALEY GREEN 18

As can be seen from the map there is a certain amount of roadwalking, but in fact, the only uninspiring section for the country admirer is the last part into Caddington.

Caddington Green is the setting-out place, away from the church past Heathfield Lower School,then at the left hand bend in the housing area look for a passageway to the side of some garages, and the path is between houses and hedges. A road is crossed, and there is no mistaking the path for it brings you out at the edge of a school playing field. Although the perimeter fence has seen better days, keep outside on the true course beside the ends of the gardens. A playing field is met on one of the bends and this time continue on the field side, following the boundary and turning two corners around a field under cultivation – the path is always there so this presents no complications in reality.

Proceed along the right hand boundary until a stile is crossed and traverse the next small pasture – there might be cattle here – then over another stile beside a low pylon into a short lane. This brings you out in front of 'The Harrow' pub in Slip End, just by a fine row of knapped flint cottages where you cross the road. Between the pub and a pair of semi-detached houses is a path (even if you think you are about to knock on the front door!), and so through the hedges into a field marked by a pair of short stout posts. Forward through the field past the double hedge screening a car parking site and out onto the road, having climbed over another stile and down between houses – you cannot get lost.

On the far side of the road is a footpath sign for Pepperstock ½ mile, and so it is down the dip slope following a line of railway sleepers with a great broad field stretching out on your right, an extensive wood as its backdrop. Passing the end of this private wood onto a broad bridleway at the white Keepers Cottage, turn right towards Markyate. The long wood belt is your company until eventually you make a descent into a bend which shelters the local sewerage works, and then up a fairly steep slope past a coppiced woodland on your left. Don't be put off by any gunfire, for the area has a clay pigeon shooting range.

Several small 'cover' woods dot the fields and the hedgerows are mainly intact, so it is a rewarding sight for those who love trees, and we owe our gratitude to the landowners for retaining them – such an English countryside feature.

In recent times the bridleway at the top of the slope has come under management, with saplings shaped and encouraged, also the hedges controlled but of generous proportions, not hacked back. With the seasonal changes in the leaves it's pleasant here all the year round. Then onto the road and down a steep hill arriving at Markyate's bypass, but be careful for cars can suddenly appear.

Cross the road by the footbridge and up the sliproad into the High Street, looking at the architectural features of this linear village with its full complement of shops. There are window frames, doorcases, a variety of brickwork, and a Victorian fire-station, all giving it a distinctive identity. Think of all the horsedrawn coaches and subsequent motor traffic that poured through the narrow street before the coming of the motorway. The old name is in fact, Market Street, and Street like the other national town name of -chester, implies Roman origins.

Leave in the direction of Dunstable and cross the bypass, taking the B4540 Luton Road which skirts the 'cut-off church' set in the end of Markyate Cell park. (The Cell is in fact a large Tudor house on the site of a nunnery). Follow the flint and brick string-course wall up the hill past a tree belt, turning left at the side road named Caddington Common. This contains a few houses, but otherwise is a tree-fringed country road passing the Beechurst riding stables, then reaching a tee junction close to Hill Farm. But our way is left down a dip and round a bend in the direction of Dunstable. Trees stand several deep through this area, not just the odd one or two brought on in a hedge.

Watch out for the footpath sign some 250 yards from the last bend, indicating right up a slope alongside a fence bordering a row of young staked trees. Simply stay alongside the right hand hedge up to the post without its finger board, and forward by the line of solitary trees, looking lost without their hedgerow. There is now a dog-leg on the alignment of the missing hedges where only a bank remains, and then forwards down a good headland path with a full grown hedge on your left hand side as the road is approached.

The return is a road walk turning left still in the country and right up Little Green Lane, being careful of vehicles, then joining the main village road lined with bungalows, and so out onto the village green with a fine view of the church ahead.

Seventy Million Years and all that

Places included: DUNSTABLE - CADDINGTON

Length of walk: 5½ miles.

Grid Ref: Sheet 166 031215

Parking: Cul-de-sac at end of Half Moon Lane near start.

Bus services: 250. Alight in Jardine Way and cross stile into Blows Downs.

Public Houses: Pubs in Dunstable, The Cricketers (Caddington).

Walk Links: Caddington Green is the start of Walk 18, and Beech Road at the southern end of Dunstable has the Walk 23 start easily reached.

Notes 1: Binoculars are useful in determining features northwards over Dunstable and Luton and beyond.

SEVENTY MILLION YEARS AND ALL THAT

Geologically speaking, the Chiltern Hills area is quite young, being of some 150 million years in a time scale of 6,000 million years. Below the earth's crust are found the sedimentary and metamorphic layers in a state of continuous movement in the zones of plate tectonics. And beneath these rocks, before encountering the mantle, the core layers around the centre are also forever restless.

The extensive layers that make up the Chiltern Hills were formed from countless billions of minute marine organisms, making this soft sedimentary limestone termed chalk. The Cretaceous Period of the calcium carbonates lasted 70 million years, when the rivers flowed slowly leaving behind sediments of shells and muds (clays). Elsewhere the major mountain-building of the Rockies and Andes were on the move, though the Himalayas and Alps were thrust up 100 million years later. At this time the climates were relatively mild, so the Cretaceous Period saw the accelerating evolution of trees, plants and insects, with the dinosaurs dominant on land and ichthyosaurs ruling the seas. Birds in a primitive form were present, and in this period small mammals emerged.

A vertical slice through the hills reveals underneath the chalk layers, sands and clays which are exposed in the vales abutting the scarp slopes. The clunch

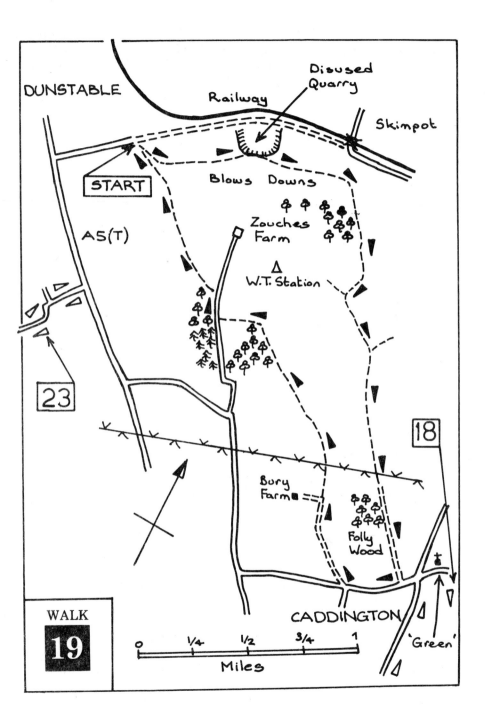

DUNSTABLE

Disused Quarry

Railway

Skimpot

START

Blows Downs

A5(T)

Zouches Farm

Δ W.T. Station

23

18

Bury Farm

Folly Wood

CADDINGTON

'Green'

WALK
19

0   1/4   1/2   3/4   1
Miles

89

Totternhoe stone is also found in pockets. Next comes the Lower Chalk aged 136 million years, with the Middle and Upper Chalk which has flints, then the cappings of clay-with-flints of the brickmaking industry; finally there are the gravels, alluvial and aeolian small deposits as soils. Inevitably ice, melting waters, wind and frost-shatter all played a part in shaping these Chiltern Hills, then with the subsidence of Europe in later ages the layers of chalk dipped southeast, exposing the flanks for weathering as steep scarps.

These gently folded hills feature dry valleys of combes and bottoms. The short, springy turf formed the basis of extensive sheep-rearing, supplanted in the twentieth century by large, hedgeless fields of corn. Woodlands, particularly in the northern hills, are generally on the steeper slopes, except where found on the younger mantle clays.

WALK

DUNSTABLE, CADDINGTON

Enter the open space of Blows Downs at the end of Half Moon Lane by means of a small gate alongside the bridleway heading in the direction of Luton. Make for the skyline which appears as a cluster of humps, using a clearly defined path (which doubles as a sledging-run in winter-time), and passing under the grid on the way. On reaching the summit, a grand vista over Dunstable and Houghton Regis is gained. Both parish churches can be seen and there are extensive views to the horizon, though the factories below and carpets of housing estates are not visually rewarding.

The grazing land on the hilltop is private, but this does not affect the walk as the direction is towards Luton. On the edge of the brow a fenced off scrubland area is soon met with a stile and a footpath beyond, just below the crest. Continue on the path staying nearest to the top fence, as variations and undulations will be met. It passes along the top rim of a disused chalk quarry, which at one time had lime-burning kilns and a rail access. The single track Dunstable to Luton line will be seen several times at the foot of the slopes, and eventually the complex of the Luton and Dunstable hospital comes into view just this side of the M1 motorway, and beyond is the broad expanse of north Luton. Stop when you are in line with the Skimpot road bridge, and the extension path rises up the slope through the bushes just in front of a stile in the fence in front of you. Do not cross but take a right turn over a stile which is to be found in a small cleft in the same alignment as the Skimpot path.

Up the shallow cleft on the path which passes by the left hand end (eastern) of the private wood, keeping the low hedge on your right. NB. It is important to follow on the correct side of the hedges as you can go completely adrift in wrong fields, especially if it is misty. Pass onto the intersection of hedges and field access gaps, this time on the right hand side of a hedge with intermittent trees, still in the same general direction. After a while ignore a sharp left turn, but go through the gap in a hedge bank and turn sharp right following the hedgerow bank. Pass through and cross the next field, and on meeting the distant hedgerow, turn left up to the top corner of a small golf course. Walk between the ditch and fairway on your left and the tall hedgerow on your right, then just before a golf course the route divides. Leave by the grassy gap on your right and follow the left hedge to the wood ahead. On the way the path switches to the other side of the hedge where there is an offset. The path then fringes the wood and enters a lane beside a caravan site, later becoming Folly Lane with houses on one side; and so arriving out onto Caddington Green, with the fine church nearby.

Leave Caddington on the Dunstable road which descends past the scout headquarters and is joined by Mancroft Road, and enter the green lane opposite through the tubular steel gates. This is a recognised bridleway for Bury Farm; actually it is a metalled surface track between banks, in fact part of the roadway for Aley Green in the other direction. Go forward then at the point where the bridleway turns down to the farm and continue onwards along the top of the bank, as the way may be choked with undergrowth.

Shortly the path enters a small wood; go in for a short distance, looking out for the exit on your left hand side. Sharp right when in the field and stay on the boundary, continuing to skirt round the end of the field and making for the power lines crossing the countryside on poles. At the top right hand corner leave the field and strike out across the open area (which might have a crop), in a north-west direction towards the place where the power line proceeds alongside the wood in front – there may be a pathway across this particular field. On arrival on the far side by this wood a grassy track there is used, then at the end corner bear left using a track alongside on the right of a tree-lined bank which is sometimes ploughed out. This brings you out onto the road for Zouches Farm and also the Wireless Telegraphy tower with its array of horns, cones and dishes which has dominated the whole walk.

Use the road towards the farm and before much longer a broad gap at the end of this last wood has a path diagonally across a field in the direction of Dunstable, as we are above the London Road with Manshead School at the foot of the slope. A fenced gap is easily located in the boundary near a small tree; proceed forwards in the cleared pathway passing over a path along the ridgetop. The path stays on a contour through the hawthorns, coming out on the open downs. Follow the brow on the scarp edge meeting up with the outgoing path, and so return.

This latter section affords views over south Dunstable and Kensworth, with Studham beyond.

Landscape in General

Places included: STUDHAM - JOCKEY END (GADDESDEN ROW)

Length of walk: 5 miles.

Grid Ref: Sheet 166 031157

Parking: Sewerage works entrance at eastern end of greens, or in the village, extending the start and finish of the walk by walking around the greens.

Bus services: 43.

Public Houses: The Bell Inn (Studham), The Red Lion (Studham).

Walk Links: Walk 21 starts by the village shops on the edge of the green. Minor road at eastern end of Bollingdon Bottom leads to Gaddesden Row, close by start of Walk 22.

Notes 1: The undulations and woods make this a very pleasant Sunday walk which can be shortened at the Beechwood Farm lane intersection, but then you will be missing the magnificent beeches of Bollingdon Bottom.

LANDSCAPE IN GENERAL

With the growth of towns into the 'green belts' the countryside is no longer in a sacrosanct position, and taken as a whole is under threat even from its guardians, the government. As soon as one steps out of a car this state of affairs is apparent, though the unpracticed eye may need alerting.

For instance, few village ponds remain. 'Save our Pond' campaigns are known, raising money for the repuddling with clay stopping the seepage; the lowering water table, as a result of massive national water consumption, may mean that the spring has to be rediscovered. Many woods of varying sizes have disappeared, where no replanting schemes are planned. By Bedfordshire County Council's own admission (and no doubt neighbouring councils will admit the same), many of the remaining woodlands are, unfortunately, neglected despite the best intentions. The 'Landscape and Wildlife' publication by Bedfordshire County Council shows that some remedial conservation measures are in progress, with room for widespread volunteer involvement.

Sadly, the one great landscape feature, the hedgerow, continues to be destroyed wholesale, its removal paid for to make way for big, intensively

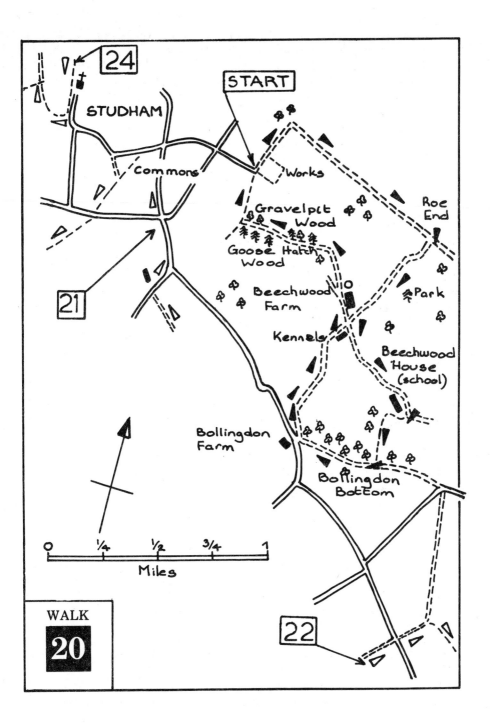

24

START

STUDHAM

Commons

Works

Gravelpit Wood

Roe End

Goose Hatch Wood

21

Beechwood Farm

Park

Kennels

Beechwood House (school)

Bollingdon Farm

Bollingdon Bottom

0   ¼   ½   ¾   1
Miles

WALK

20

22

cultivated fields, whose produce sometimes merely adds to European grain stockpiles. The reader may point out that most of our hedges are the result of the Enclosure Acts mostly 200 years ago, but we formerly enjoyed extensive woodlands and commons to supply most of our needs and these areas are now in a very shrunken state. Grubbed-out hedges with their trees are a net loss, offset only by new tree shelter belts around quarries.

Hedges serve a myriad functions well worth listing at this juncture. Firstly, as biological 'gene banks' in the foremost position; as habitats for birds, animals, insects and invertebrates; as 'highways' and foodchains for wildlife, now that fields are lacking in natural food; and as refuges for many botanical species. As many as 284 different invertebrates alone use oak trees as a host. These hedges also prevent soil erosion, do service as a windbreak, prevent water from being soaked up, retard 'soil creep' on hillsides where roots no longer exist to bind the soil, and offer shade to help retain moisture in the fields. More than thirty five common but vital shrubs and trees can be found in our hedgerows.

109,000 miles of hedges have been eradicated since 1947, ie. 22% of the total mileage, and they continue to disappear at the rate of 4,000 miles a year according to government figures. A 'dying landscape', in the words of a Cambridge countryside historian, Oliver Rackham.

Another adversity our hedges must face is the effect of chemical spraying in the fields, leaching into the root systems and the water-table. Then there is the practice of stubble-burning which can cause scorching, though this problem has admittedly eased now that edge ploughing must be undertaken first.

STUDHAM, JOCKEY END, (GADDESDEN ROW)

The walk commences at the clock-tower on the Green, leaving the village in an easterly direction and following the roadside along the common; on reaching the crossroads take the service road ahead. We start leaving the open common land, and hereabouts trees and bushes make an appearance, then shortly we arrive at the gates of the local sewage works – don't be deterred! An excellent tree-lined green lane is discovered on the left ascending a slope, then after a short distance a sharp right hand bend is encountered.

The straight broad section ahead is easy going on high ground, with fields near at hand and woods in the middle distance on either side, so there are views to be enjoyed.

On reaching the hard-surfaced road at Roe End, turn to the right by the Gt Gaddesden sign in front of the flint house, onto a well-defined stone track. It descends down a gentle slope, with a wood alongside on your right, which becomes a tree-lined lane. Before long a crossing is met; turn left here passing an attractive brick and flint built house. Fences mark the way, and a concrete bungalow of the 1940s vintage is met; continue on the drive which passes in front of Beechwood House (now a school).

Where the driveway bears left to the school entrance your direction is to continue forward into the area of the service buildings, towards the house that leads out onto the playing fields of the school. Now follow the boundary wall at your right hand side, then at the end of the wall cross over the narrow green fairway by turning sharp left. A cedar tree on the edge of the woodland will be found, then use the path on its left side. However, it should be noted that paths hereabouts do change in the wood, either due to clearance or through avoiding fallen trees. Make due south (directly away from the house) through the woods, the path usually being fairly clear, then on reaching the fence cross at the special wooden section into a field, make for a similar one at the bottom right hand end and so enter Bollingdon Bottom.

In the summer months it is a dry, sunken, beech-lined lane and a very pleasant spot. But in the wet it can be muddy if either horse or motorcycle riders have churned it up. Here we turn right and walk its length until the outlet into Jockey End is reached.

Jockey End has a collection of timber-framed buildings around a longish green which is up the road on your left; they are not all in view but do make the diversion and look about – besides there is a very convenient pub in the corner.

At the road there is a good track immediately sharp right, rising fairly steeply and passing a farm with cattle-rearing provisions in covered stockyards. As you go on there are views across to the rear of Beechwood School, then, soon after passing another small wood on your left, the crossing of the ways is encountered again.

Now turn left past Beechwood Farm, built on the old 'model' lines, and on into the plantation, bearing right at the fork – the left track is private. Several side 'rides' will be encountered but just keep on the main clearway, which after a while bears slightly left. Note any signs stating no throughway.

Eventually – half a mile or so – a field is reached at the boundary fence. Here turn right and follow the field round, coming out into the top south-eastern corner of the common on the slope above the sewerage works entrance. Walk along the top of the common by the hedge and over to the road, with the high ground affording extensive distant views. Near the road is a favourite spot for model aircraft enthusiasts. Simply return into Studham itself, with the church seen amongst the trees away on the left foreground.

Studham boasts two pubs well known in the locality – the Red Lion on the green and the Bell a short way up the Whipsnade/Dunstable road.

Fields – Man Controls Nature

Places included: STUDHAM - HUDNALL - GT GADDESDEN

Length of walk: 7½ miles.

Grid Ref: Sheet 166 023157

Parking: Discreet parking beside the common.

Bus services: 43.

Public Houses: The Bell Inn (Studham), The Red Lion (Studham), Cock & Bottle (Gt Gaddesden).

Walk Links: Walk 20 starts at the eastern end of common. Gt Gaddesden is close by the turning point of Walk 22 at Water End along the River Gade. Short road walk from Hudnall connects with Little Gaddesden near the Adelaide Brownlow memorial.

Notes 1: The headwaters of the Gade Valley are encountered before entering urban areas, and the walker may like to compare with the Lea Valley.

FIELDS – MAN CONTROLS NATURE

Unbelievable though it may sound, most of our countryside is man-made. Little of the primeval land exists, even some moorland came about by the denudation encouraged by man through the grazing of sheep. The fields, hedges, and most woods show man's work, even rivers were altered for milling and navigation, and more recently by the water authorities. Add to this the intrusions of roads, canals, rail and buildings of every description, and the point is made.

Lynchets, the earliest surviving prehistoric cultivation, seen as terraced agriculture on hillsides in the Chilterns, can readily be found in the countryside, but not a lot is known about these early lifestyles. Practical experiments reliving those times in as realistic a manner as possible, using simulated tooling and comparable animal breeds, yielded considerable revelations. On the Buster site, housing based on post-hole archaeological evidence provided the basis for this latter-day community which attempted the re-creation of the ancient agricultural methods and plot cultivation.

With the coming of written history, records indicate that the earliest regular agriculture was a two 'field' system, one being in cultivation and the

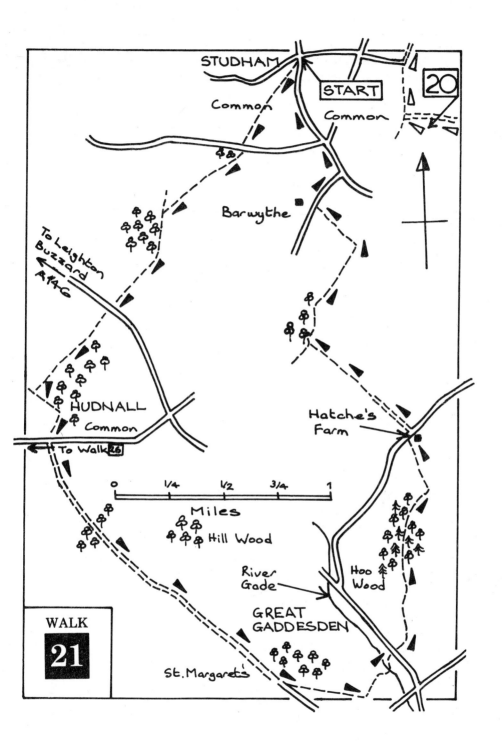

STUDHAM

START

20

Common

Common

Barwythe

To Leighton
Buzzard
A146

HUDNALL
Common

To Walk 20

Hatche's
Farm

0   1/4   1/2   3/4   1
Miles

Hill Wood

River
Gade

Hoo
Wood

GREAT
GADDESDEN

St. Margaret's

WALK
21

other fallow. When more land came into cultivation from patch clearance, a three field system evolved, with their scattered strips tilled by the tied labour of the feudal period. Wastelands still served as lands for wood gathering 'by hook and crook', for pig-pannage and pasturage, not forgetting that great areas remained untouched except as royal and aristocratic hunting grounds. The ridge and furrow lands seen in many meadows are a legacy from the teams of oxen (not to be confused with the effects of steam-ploughing by traction engines), and have left us with a unit of measure, the furlong.

Enclosures, though not new, accelerated in the Tudor reigns, establishing permanent hedges or drystone walling for tending these new fields, increasing the wealth of the landowners, be they for crops or sheep. Piece-meal enclosing continued for the next two centuries but via the far-reaching Enclosure Acts (1760-1820) in the reign of George III most arable lands and much of the commons and wastelands were enclosed. Much hardship resulted, with the displaced worker forced into the developing manufacturing industries or canal construction. Social history books devote many chapters to the subject of enclosures. These regularly-shaped fields, usually of five to ten acres, though they could be fifty acres if the internal hedges were not planted, had quickthorn hedges cut-and-laid into stockproof barriers. Surveyors took into account any old field systems, access lanes, natural features, commons and glebe lands, not forgetting the earlier enclosures, which explains why we now see irregular fields. Many twisting rural roads stem from the enclosures! Thus were ushered in new patterns of life in the country with the increasing pace of mechanisation from the Corn Law Acts onwards.

WALK

21

STUDHAM, HUDNALL, GT GADDESDEN.

Cross the road and enter the open woodland which runs parallel to the road going out to Studham church. Through the bracken and down the slope to the old school building which is now a private house. The path up the slope across an arable field to the left of the schoolhouse is usually left intact by the farmer, and meets the road in front of the houses. (Don't take the path beside the schoolhouse). On the other side of the road at Bury Farm, the footpath sign points the way between the hedges of two houses. Cross over the gate or stile at the end. Bear right across an open field and then through a gateway, making for the trees on the far edge of the field. Now onto the bridleway south into the edge of the wood in front and out at the far end. Follow the trees on your left, then when you are in the hill meadow overlooking the Gade Valley commence descending the slope.

Go over the barbed wire fencing in the bankside and descend the hill, keeping the remnant hedgerow at your right hand side. It is now a simple matter of reaching the road, having first gone through the gate of the last field.

The trackway on the other side of the road is very clear and rises into the woodland of Hudnall Common, next joining a service road which is followed leftwards. Pass into the drive of some very desirable residences on the other side of the Common road, and here we have some beautiful woodlands with the drive petering out into a trackway which in wet weather may contain large full-width puddles. Continue undeterred, for the views along this ridge are of countryside scattered with small pockets of woodland. May the farmers long preserve these and the hedgerows.

It is quite straightforward through here, on a quite well-surfaced track beyond the sticky section, passing by St Margaret's Farm and school, then keep a lookout for the footpath sign pointing down into the valley just above a small wood on the left side. As a general direction make for the left end of the houses below, first crossing over a low hedge and continuing down the left side of the next field.

This leads into a long, narrow, green field which has a stile/gateway exit on the left into the water meadow. Circle round the wide stretch of water of the dammed River Gade and cross by the causeway and bridge, coming out at the stile. Over the road and follow the right hand hedge, then diagonally across an open field on a well defined path, rising uphill into the bottom corner of the wood ahead. It is a pleasant mixed woodland, with open spaces worth visiting any time of the year, with a straightforward path in front – ignore the right hand path on entering the wood. The exit out of the wood is by means of two stiles close to each other into a hill meadow overlooking the Gade Valley. Remain close to the right hand line of trees and pass through the gate and follow the left hand edge of the next field, entering the last one through some wire-fencing shortly before reaching the road.

Turn right, and on reaching Hatches Farm take the minor road left at the tee junction, which eventually peters out into a broad stony track with hedges on either side. This leads via a gateway into more fields, then at the tree belt the next path marker is found. When this terminates cross onto the right hand boundary of the left hand field and continue round the corner of the field, eventually arriving at Barwithe, a house set in woods near the road.

It is now a road walk back onto the common. First turn right out onto the road, then left at the tee junction, crossing over the crossroads which takes you out onto the common. Remember to stay on the right hand side on roads.

'Them Thar Hills'

Places included: GADDESDEN ROW - STAGS END - WATER END - GADDESDEN PLACE

Length of walk: 6 miles.

Grid Ref: Sheet 166 050129

Parking: Gaddesden Row school vicinity.

Bus services: 43.

Public Houses: The Plough (Gaddesden Row), The Red Lion (Water End).

Walk Links: The turning point at Water End is close by Gt Gaddesden on Walk 21 up the River Gade.

Notes 1: A walk with plenty of variety of scenery.

2: Paths around Gaddesden Place may be rerouted with slight deviations.

'THEM THAR HILLS'

From Pitstone through to the Telegraph Hill the northern Chilterns are bare compared to the beech-hangers on the hills around High Wycombe and Missenden. These woods north of the River Thames were a source of material for the chair-makers – locally known as 'bodgers' – who with their pole-lathes turned chair legs and shaped the seats. Displays in High Wycombe museum depict aspects of the trade and working conditions in the woods. These northern hills supported sheep.

The North and South Downs may be considered the nearest in character to the Chilterns, whilst the bare Berkshire Downs are in sharp contrast, yet all are basically chalk hills.

Travelling about the country we realise that the British isles is fortunate in being so well-endowed with hill systems of widely differing nature.

Limestone gives rise to other sets of hills, the Cotswolds being the best known, where woods gain a hold on the steep slopes and drystone walling replaces the familiar hedges of the Home Counties. Limestone scenery appears again in Derbyshire's Peak District and in the Pennine Uplands, the result of geological faulting where water seepage forms subterranean caverns under the

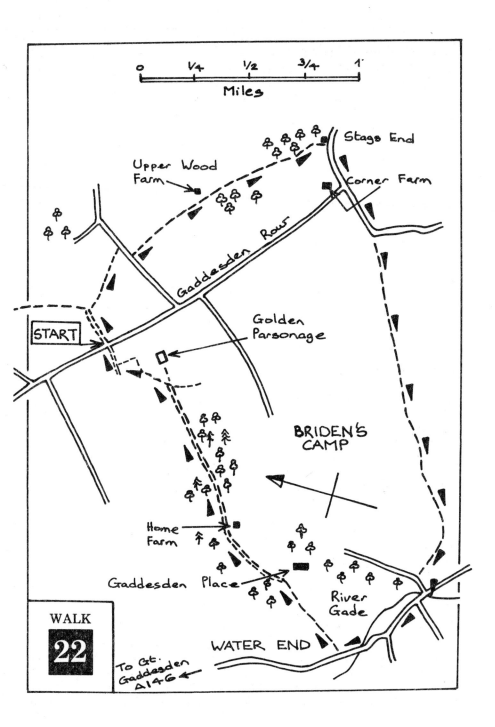

Miles

Stags End

Upper Wood Farm

Corner Farm

Gaddesden Row

START

Golden Parsonage

BRIDEN'S CAMP

Home Farm

Gaddesden Place

River Gade

WATER END

WALK
22

To Gt. Gaddesden A146

hilltops of a bleak and moorland terrain. Chalk is the major stratum in the 'folded' downland hills of Dorset overlying Wealden beds, whilst erosion of the Portland and Purbeck limestones created the unique coastline scenery. Heathlands on the 'poor' sand and gravel topsoils allow heathers and acid-tolerant trees – usually coniferous – to take hold.

As a total contrast in scenery the Dartmoor hills are made of granite, slates and sandstones bearing no trees; however Devonshire's valleys contain fertile farmlands.

GADDESDEN ROW, STAGS END, WATER END, GADDESDEN PLACE

By the school in Gaddesden Row is a good spot for parking a car, and it is here that the sign showing Flamstead 2½ miles is followed. Down through the fields for ½ mile and a bridleway junction is met. The direction is right keeping the hedge on your right hand side, then out onto the roads.

Right at the road and after about 100 yards left at the bridleway sign and on to Upper Wood Farm. Cross over the rickyard and continue along green lanes which skirt small woods into Stags End – a very pleasant stretch of countryside. The horse centre stands on a corner, so be careful in case of the occasional vehicle.

Bear right on the road, passing the very trim Corner Farm which marks the end of Gaddesden Row. Continue ahead along the sign-posted Hemel Hempstead road and enter a tree lined bridleway in front of you on a very sharp left hand bend in the road. Walk into the bridleway keeping the hedge always at your right hand side and the built-up outskirts of Hemel Hempstead can be clearly seen. From this high ground one is rewarded with views along the Gade Valley, with the church spire of Old Hemel Church seen in the distance.

Pass through the pedestrian gate and progress past a small wood on your left hand, then on downhill under the overhead power line and out to the A4146 at the Red Lion public house.

This stretch of the valley is very attractive and much photographed, with the wide stretches of water and clusters of trees making it a much frequented haunt of motorists. Follow the river banks up to the celebrated Water End bridge and cottages, where the slow flowing water was used for beds of watercress cultivation.

Continue on the road past the lead-windowpaned cottages with their attractive tiled roofs, arriving at a phone box on the edge of the hamlet. Near the two white country houses cross a stile which is just out of sight behind the roadside wall where the footpath sign indicates Gaddesden Row, and proceed directly uphill straight forward in the direction of the stile set in a fence slightly to the left of the porticoed Gaddesden Place House. This path is usually well defined since it is used by many ramblers. Keeping diagonally left across the hilltop under trees; it is worth looking backwards here along the length of the valley.

Make for and cross the stile in the boundary fence, then follow this fence which encloses the parkland. On reaching the end of this wooded area make for the asbestos roofs of Home Farm set amongst the trees.

The path should enter the wood on the left of the pond, but if it is overgrown enter the wood just after the pond where it becomes a plantation alongside farmbuildings. Stay on the path close to the farm.

This then leads into the well-made farm road through the fields leading out to a red brick residence built in the Queen Anne style called Golden Parsonage. On approaching look out for the footpath sign pointing to the left, and thereby skirt the field in a quarter circle. At a point opposite the front door of the Parsonage cross the fence, then right over a stile and sharp left – careful as this turn may not be noticed in the hedgerow.

Make for the wood ahead and on arriving at the driveway of the restored period house use the drive for the last section and complete the excursion.

Chalk – the Unsung Mineral in the Service of Man

Places included: DUNSTABLE - KENSWORTH

Length of walk: 5 miles.

Grid Ref: Sheet 166 032204

Parking: Beech Road.

Bus services: 43, 245 and 343.

Public Houses: The Glider (Lowther Road, Dunstable), The Highwayman (London Road, Dunstable), The Farmer's Boy (Kensworth), The Old Red Lion (Kensworth).

Walk Links: Can be combined with Walk 22 whose start is not far away. Also, by walking out to Whipsnade Common at the church a mile away on the B4540 road the middle section of Walk 24 is reached.

Notes 1: This walk is all on roads though undulating, so take care as cars come unexpectedly. However, this is the best walk in the book for those who have done no walking at all as it is fully flexible, starting where you wish and for as far as you wish, with a car always at hand.

2: Kensworth is a village with four 'ends', viz. Church End, Kensworth Common, Kensworth Lynch and Kensworth Watling Street.

CHALK – THE UNSUNG MINERAL IN THE SERVICE OF MAN

If ever there was a subject waiting for an author in the popular social history book world, then chalk fills that bill – now that may appear a strange statement. Cement, lime, whiting and clunch all originate from chalk (calcium carbonate), with flints as a by-product. Despite all the great chalk quarries in the South Bedfordshire area, hardly a word can be found, except a mention in reports and schools' mineral studies. Yet Houghton Regis in particular can be considered a small town sitting on the edge of a huge cement-producing complex. Sundon and Totternhoe had extensive workings, and quarrying continues in Kensworth, while Pitstone still quarries and converts chalk into cement. Mineral rail-lines for tipping, plus tubes, conveyors and overhead bucket-cableways were features of the scene.

Lime-making entails baking lumps of chalk in a bottle-kiln, producing a white caustic alkaline powder for liming fields, or it is hydrated by adding water

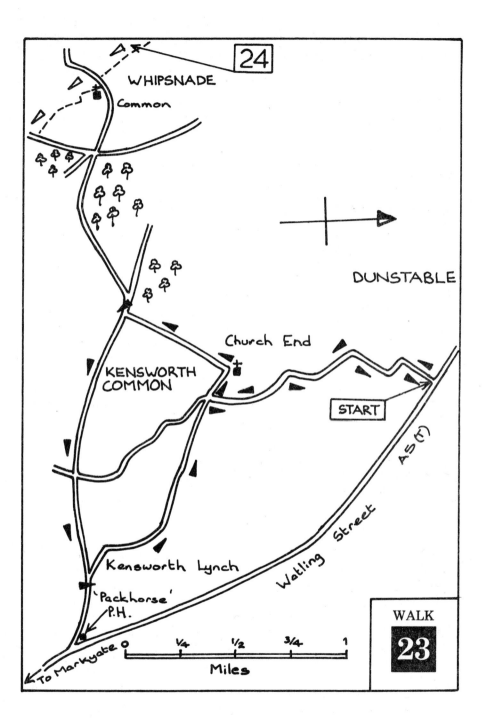

WHIPSNADE

Common

24

DUNSTABLE

Church End

KENSWORTH
COMMON

START

KENSWORTH

A 5 (T)

Watling Street

Kensworth Lynch

'Packhorse'
P.H.

To Markyate

0   ¼   ½   ¾   1

Miles

WALK
23

and used for concrete in the construction industry. Totternhoe still has lime works.

Cement making uses crushed chalk made into a slurry which is fed into the top end of a rotating inclined kiln, fired from the lower end. Cement lumps fall out which are then crushed into a powder to be bagged or bulk-delivered by rail or road. Slurry from the Kensworth quarry, incidentally, is pumped to Rugby for firing in their kilns.

Seven works at one time made whiting in Dunstable. In this process the chalk was crushed and again mixed with water, but this time fed into large brick-lined settling tanks set in the ground. Eventually the chalk settled as a sediment and any stones present sank to the bottom. When the separation was completed, the water was drained off and the mud dried out for later digging-out and wheelbarrowing into the yard. The residue was shaped into cakes or rolls and placed on large stones in drying sheds with a final drying on the top of brick ovens. These rolls of whiting found uses in lining playing fields, in decorating, as fillers for rubber manglerollers, in toothpaste and in the bad old days, as a filler for flour.

Totternhoe clunch stone does not weather well, so has been used for church interiors especially as it carved very easily, and in the locality could be found as the lining material for cellars. Clunch is no longer extracted, but being right at the bottom of the chalk levels was mined working from 'driftways' and the blocks hauled out on trolleys. Totternhoe was last worked in the 19th century, though the galleries were in existence up into this century.

Invariably, where there is chalk, there is flint, those steel-grey silica lumps with a white crusting. Besides being split and used as a means for making sparks for lighting and guns, early man mined specifically for them and shaped them into tools. Nowadays flints are mostly seen in a knapped state as a building material, though not for new houses. Since flints are not suitable to be used for the corners of houses, these will always be of brick quoins, as will the window and doorways.

WALK

23

DUNSTABLE, KENSWORTH

Leave on Beech Road, Dunstable, opposite the Hertfordshire BTR factory by the Glenwood School for handicapped children and the redundant Priory Hospital – which served the town for many years, firstly as a cottage hospital, then for isolation cases and latterly for the care of the elderly. There is a steep rise beyond the Lowther Road turning, then walk beside the dominant row of beech trees and finally, round the next bend on to the crest. Beware cars, for you are hidden from drivers. The fenced-off, artificial mound is in fact a concrete water reservoir, and on this level stretch of road, St Albans Abbey and N. London are visible. This twisting road following field boundaries has a number of ups and downs, eventually descending in a sunken section into Kensworth Church End crossroads.

As many of the walks described are clockwise, for a change we will make the next loop anti-clockwise by going round past a row of cottages and a farm, meeting up with the flint church back on a rise in a most attractive setting. Directly away from the church is the next part on a road that initially rises and then falls away sharply across a vale and steeply upwards into the top end of Kensworth. Although dry, this area falling away from Dunstable Downs provides the headwaters of the River Ver seen along the St Albans valley.

We find ourselves close by the zoo traffic turnoff, whilst we now head for the A5 down the village. Look out for Grove Farm with its mullioned windows in a nucleated series of buildings. Nearby are the school and non-conformist churches, making an interesting study about village development; indeed there is a group locally researching the subject. Stay on the road at the Studham crossing then down the slope into Kensworth Lynch, which is a hairpin bend left. Here the buildings of mature age and character are sympathetically improved; watch for the grills in the wall of the last residence on the right round the bend, a sure indication of flooding tendencies in times past. We leave the Lynch near a pair of farms, walking on the road that is now in a deep hollow, before gently rising up onto the crossroads met earlier. The return presents no problems: it's the right hand road.

Conservation Areas – in Towns

Places included: DUNSTABLE DOWNS - WHIPSNADE - STUDHAM

Length of walk: 6½ miles.

Grid Ref: Sheet 166 008197

Parking: Adequate parking space near Information Centre.

Bus services: Nil.

Public Houses: The Chequers (Whispnade), The Bell Inn (Studham), The Red Lion (Studham).

Walk Links: Walk 1 passes through the first section of this walk.

Notes 1: Many views of the animals in Whipsnade Zoo can be seen during this walk, which either passes through or has woodlands always in sight.

CONSERVATION AREAS – IN TOWNS

Conservation in towns can prove a very emotional topic, provoking or stimulating nostalgia and off-the-cuff views on what 'they' should be doing. It does not occur to the pontificators that they themselves should be involved, instead of adopting the easy option of criticising others. Nicolas Pevsner wrote an appreciation of just about every important building in the country, providing the groundwork for John Betjeman and Alec Clifton-Taylor, sadly both with us no more. They, and others, preached the appreciation of our old buildings in TV programmes and books. Less well known are the submissions before the Inquiries and Planning Departments, making cases for saving some of our heritage from the developers.

Most towns now have trails linking the important buildings and giving historical thumbnail sketches. Seldom do the architectural merits, the social history consequences or vernacular explanations get a mention. Writers think that the public can only absorb simplistic, self-evident subjects.

Look above the shopfronts to see what is at first floor level and whether it has an old roof. Walks in the side roads of both towns and villages can be very revealing, and one puzzles as to why buildings are where they are, and what sort of influences and materials were employed. The features can be a visual delight, so may I suggest a few that can be sought in the conservation areas of Dunstable and Luton? Parapets, double-pile buildings with 'M' roofs, doorcases, drip-

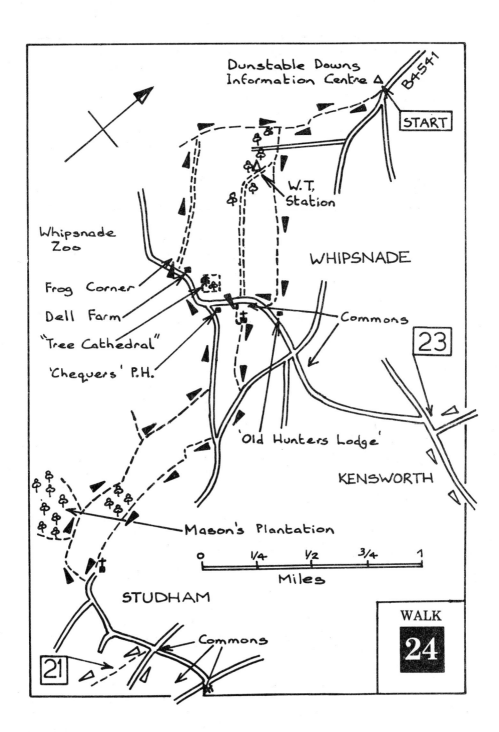

Dunstable Downs
Information Centre △

B4541

START

W.T.
Station

WHIPSNADE

Whipsnade
Zoo

Frog Corner

Dell Farm

"Tree Cathedral"

'Chequers' P.H.

Commons

23

'Old Hunters Lodge'

KENSWORTH

Mason's Plantation

0   ¼   ½   ¾   1
Miles

STUDHAM

Commons

21

WALK
24

hoods, sash windows, coal holes and cellars, outside wash-houses and privies, fanlights, plum and red contrasting brickwork, workshops and much more. The more we probe the more we realise how big is the story of evolution of a township.

Groupings of buildings in the conservation areas have some significance as part of the townscape contributing towards its character, yet on their own they might almost be dismissed. Councils and planners that do not have a feel for the past show a lack of sympathy for their role as custodians, leading them to commit some almighty blunders.

This is an age of change, when buildings come and go almost without our realising, eg. the 'Windsock', a modern pub in Dunstable. So take another look at the churches, cemeteries, villas, conversions of all sorts, and you could be in for a few surprises.

Though these comments have been directed mainly at the towns, villages and the rural areas are also experiencing change and have their own stories to tell.

WALK

24

DUNSTABLE DOWNS, WHIPSNADE, STUDHAM

From the Information Centre on Dunstable Downs go along the top of the downs in the direction of Ivinghoe Beacon, entering a belt of scrubland on a broad path. Then at the far end take the top edge of the long field you are now in, where the path leads along a band of mature beech trees and brings you out at a bridleway now in good condition. After a few hundred yards enter the sunken path on the boundary and cross the Chute Farm road. A roadway will be encountered in the woodland serving as access for the aerial mast and coming directly from Whipsnade Common, but this is not used. Instead proceed forward keeping the woodland on your R.H.S. and moving directly away from the Downs; shortly the green lane passes between fields with the one on your right recently come into the possession of the Beds. and Hunts. Wildlife Trust, no doubt to be developed into a downland meadow – I hope so. In the course of time arriving on the Whipsnade Common close to the Old Hunters Lodge, the timbered 15th century restaurant.

Turn right and walk towards the Zoo, or the Whipsnade Wild Animal Park to give the new name, and take the opportunity to visit the unique Tree Cathedral by following the National Trust signs. Mr. Blyth commenced planting in 1930 (as a gesture for the peace of mankind) as a result of his own family hardships resulting from the First World War. As can be seen from the diagram the site is most impressive with something for all seasons; it is truly remarkable for the variety and layout of the trees and provides a lovely setting for the occasional services held there. No admission charges for this excellent diversion.

Whipsnade Church lies on the other side of the common. We enter the churchyard and make for the rear, leaving by the stile and traversing the next two fields. These give high ground views out to the zoo, and the railway though the rhino enclosures can be clearly seen from this vantage point. Walking along in the direction of Studham make sure you stay on the right and beware traffic. There is a descent from here and houses appear behind the hedges and trees; now watch out for a post-mounted letterbox on a minor road junction.

Into this road, which is now forbidden for vehicles, and take the path by the first bungalow on the left, which is quite clear. You will find that there are a few changes of direction on the path, which then leaves the rear of the gardens and heads directly across the fields towards a long wood across the skyline. Three smallish fields on the course, then down a dip slope beside a wood and up through the fourth field, bearing slightly left straight for Studham church set in the trees. The church is cement rendered and has a clerestory and a battlemented tower.

A broad green way takes you out onto a farm road which connects with Studham Common. As you go along keep a watch out for a track through the trees on your right, just before the bend in the road; you are only going a few

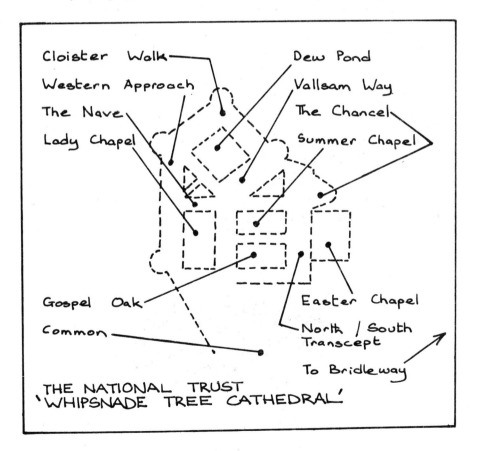

yards down this road encircling the copse. Off the road is a footpath sign, so proceed forwards with a fence on your left up by a hedge; this brings you to the edge of Mason's Plantation of 1929. Enter this delightful woodland, staying on the bridleway – in wet weather this can be on the muddy side – then after about ½ mile, while the wood continues around on the left of a boundary bend, we take a sharp right turn at the bridleway sign.

So the plantation is left behind, and we take our route along a semi-cleared hedgerow bank beside a slightly sunken old track. This once green lane passes the rear of the wood skirted earlier, and a white arrow on a post confirms our direction. Continue with the hedge still on your right, which is usually in a fairly good state, then into a wood by the bridleway sign. On the far side we come across the zoo's perimeter fence going forward not left. This stretch can be very muddy indeed, so be warned, but this is offset by the free animal viewing of antelope, rhino, and camels. (Elephants can be seen from the road at the zoo's entrance, and further along, penguins and bison at the top of Bison Hill; do make a zoo visit with your family and see everything).

The minor road at the letterbox is regained and we now see the rear of Whipsnade church. Turn left up this road in a hollow-way arriving on the common at the 'Chequers' pub. Across the common is the main entry into the Tree Cathedral; we follow the road rowards the zoo, but instead of leaving the common, descend the slope on the right and come upon the residential Dell Farm Outdoor Centre run by Bedfordshire County Council for teaching practical rural subjects to children.

Open the bridleway gate and shut it behind you. Stay on this track firstly at the rear of the zoo car park, eventually arriving on top of the downs at Bison Hill above the hidden car park. A stretch is immediately in front of you that is often used for picnics overlooking the sweep of Ashridge, the Beacon, and in the distance, Aylesbury.

To your right is a walker's gate beside a tubular steel farm-type gate. And from here, by following the right hand hedge, the line of the Downs is taken; and it is something like a mile back to the Information Centre.

The Ashridge Estates

Places included: **IVINGHOE BEACON - ASHRIDGE MONUMENT - NORTH AND WEST ASHRIDGE ESTATE LANDS**

Length of walk: 6 miles.

Grid Ref: Sheet 165 964155

Parking: Car park at entrance of Clipperdown Cottage private road or on hard-standing nearer Ivinghoe Beacon.

Bus services: 61.

Public Houses: The Greyhound (Aldbury), The Valiant Trooper .(Aldbury).

Walk Links: The main avenue (Prince's Riding) from Ashridge College through to the Monument conveniently gives the link for both Ashridge walks.

Notes 1: The B4506 road from Dagnall to Northchurch effectively bisects the estate but this should not deter you from combining Walks 25 and 26.

2: The southern quarters of the estates contain a bracken heathland and a more open terrain.

3: A map of the whole Ashridge Estate has been provided to enable walkers to devise their own additional routes (page 117).

4: Ivinghoe Beacon is popular for short distance hilltop walks giving stupendous views along the Chilterns. From the flanks of the adjacent Steps Hill the Ridgeway Walk rises towards its termination on the Beacon.

THE ASHRIDGE ESTATES

The Ashridge Estate, in the care of the National Trust for more than 60 years, comprises some 4,000 acres in the form of commons, open spaces and woodland, plus 1,200 acres of farmland. It is designated an 'area of outstanding natural beauty'.

Ivinghoe Beacon in the north affords splendid views through 360°, being 700' above sea level, its summit the site of an Iron Age settlement. The estate

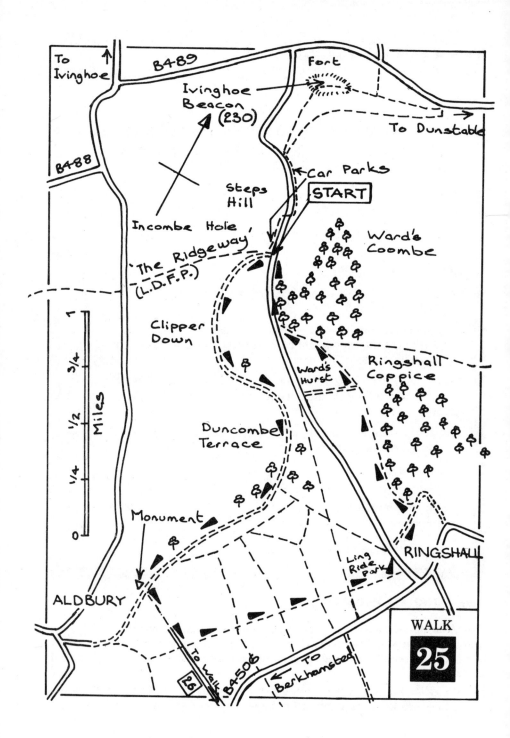

114

itself is more a continuous grouping of copse and woods of different ages, from the ancient Frithsden Beeches pollarded for centuries as a source of useful timber, to the plantations of beech, oaks, larch, sweet and Spanish chestnuts. Self-set birches can be found and much gorse. Few, if any, ash trees will be found.

Aldbury, Berkhamsted, Ringshall, Pitstone and Northchurch have all had thier commons absorbed into the estate, as sheep grazing became uneconomic in the 1930s and the commoners did not exercise their rights to the natural use of the lands for activities such as woodbote, furzecutting and pig pasturing. Ringshall Common is now colonised by birch.

At the southern extremity Berkhamsted Common overlooks the Tring Gap formed by the meltwaters of the Ice Age breaking through the Chilterns a million years ago. Now it is a valley utilised by road, canal and rail.

That justly much-photographed village of Aldbury is a short downhill walk departing from the left hand side of the Monument. From here also, by staying on the top tracks, a circular walk can be made taking in Tom's Hill and Berkhamsted Common, returning via the chequered flintworked Thunderdell Lodge at the roadside or by the northbound central path through Aldbury Common Woods.

Walks 25 and 26 are devised as an encouragement for exploratory walking in less-frequented areas of this popular parkland. The numerous paths enable visitors to make their own rambles in the future, so a general map of the estates is included for that purpose. Besides, by leaving the populous parts there is the bonus of increasing the chances of seeing fallow deer.

WALK

IVINGHOE BEACON, ASHRIDGE MONUMENT, NORTH AND WEST ASHRIDGE ESTATE LANDS

Before setting out on the walk take in the panorama of Dunstable Downs and Whipsnade seen on the distant skyline beyond the hedgelined fields around Dagnall.

The stone surfaced Clipper Down track enters beech woodlands, the glory of Ashridge, and we shall never lose sight of them throughout. With many changes of direction the way follows the top of the escarpment. The prominence of Pitstone cement works gives way to the pleasant sights of the Tring valley hills. Pass through and shut the gate at Clipperdown Cottage, and there is no mistaking the presence of the inhabitants of the kennels there!

From here onwards we are rewarded with long views through the trees which spill down the slopes, lovely particularly in the spring sunshine or in their autumnal foliage colours. Here along Duncombe Terrace the uprooted beeches show the effect of recent storm damage, the shallow rooting being a sign of thin topsoils around the roots. This area was also severely ravaged by gales in 1928. Paths in the fields below around Aldbury provide good walks girded by the woodsides of Ashridge.

Continue on the main track ignoring side-junctions and by generally bearing right a footbridge is crossed over a cleft. Pick up the yellow arrow markers leading onto the greensward at the base of the Monument. In summer months this can be climbed for a small charge, looking out from above the tree canopy. The National Trust has an Information Centre here, and donkeys in the nearby field attract children's interest. From here the Aldbury and Tom's Hill extensions start.

Leaving the Monument we set off down the metalled avenue in the direction of the distant Ashridge House/College, the subject of the next walk. Part way down, where the avenue broadens, watch out on the right for twin concrete side turnings in the form of a 'vee', almost the last of the concrete drives and pads that riddled the park when temporary huts billeted 20,000 servicemen in World War II.

On the left hand side is a greenway, confirmed by a small area of young staked saplings, and further up is a row of posts preventing car access. The way now bears slightly right through undulations, with birches as the principal tree. From now onwards if in doubt choose right, thus regaining the main road, for very few identifiers can be given and the traffic sounds afar can usually be detected. A modern carved bridleway post at an intersection is met and you can now turn left into a possibly muddy clearway. Several of these posts come into view but continue onward on a route that is parallel to the main road.

This is one of the best parts of Ashridge with young trees in an extensive coverage, enhanced by birdsong, woodpeckers away out of sight, squirrels, rabbits and most likely deer, but you must be quiet. Move slowly if you see them as they will probably dart away, their colours blending with the tree trunks. Few people frequent this area. The way finishes at the Ringshall bungalows, then by skirting on the grassy path along the bottom of the gardens the Ringshall/Beacon road is reached. Close at hand is the Ling Ride car park which has its own path direct to the Monument.

Rather than use the long roadside paths as a return, the way chosen is by means of fields near the northern boundaries of the Ashridge Estates. Look for the footpath sign on the right hand side of Ringshall Copse houses, indicating the direction up a broad rise followed by a stile, and so up a drive between high hedges through which the Little Gaddesden area is glimpsed. We pass a sad, derelict, but very striking, estate house with exaggerated high-pitched roofs worthy of restoration, but cluttered about by equally shabby caravans. On around the grass mound of a covered reservoir and out by way of the footpath-marked stile in the left hand corner. From now on the dense Ringshall Coppice is followed through three fields, contrasting pleasantly with the earlier woodland walking. Dockey Wood plantation serves as a break in the rolling scene.

Here comes a slight change in direction as we leave the woodside, following yellow arrows on a track across a pair of fields up to Ward's Hurst Farm. This is passed in an anti-clockwise manner outside the barbed wire fencing through into a field with a lot of dispersed farm equipment in varying states of disrepair. The right hand corner of Ward's Coombe Wood is a crossing of paths, for right takes one down into Dagnall and ahead is an alternative woodland path on the eastern fringes and back via the flanks of Ivinghoe Beacon. However, we go west (left) in the fields just outside the woods, arriving on the road, then by taking the path within the boundary of the wood we are on the last leg of the walk.

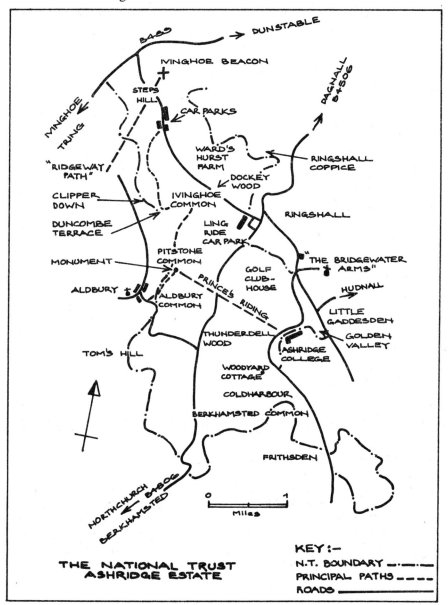

THE NATIONAL TRUST
ASHRIDGE ESTATE

KEY:—

N.T. BOUNDARY —·—·—
PRINCIPAL PATHS — — —
ROADS ——————

Ashridge House

Places included: LITTLE GADDESDEN - ASHRIDGE MANAGEMENT COLLEGE - SOUTH AND EAST ESTATE LANDS

Length of walk: 4 miles.

Grid Ref: Sheet 165 993134

Parking: Village Hall car park which is up Church Road next to the local school directly opposite Ashridge Park entrance road.

Bus services: Nil.

Public Houses: The Bridgewater Arms (Little Gaddesden).

Walk Links: The short road between Hudnall and Little Gaddesden provides a useful link with Walk 21, or alternatively the good clear paths connecting Hudnall and Little Gaddesden church offer fine valley views and prospects for future walking.

Prince's Riding, the broad avenue stretching towards the Monument from Ashridge College, connects Walks 25 and 26.

Notes 1: Parking in this part of the Ashridge Park is strictly forbidden.

2: Little Gaddesden Church is now isolated from the village, and can be seen above the Gade Valley, whilst the village re-established itself along the park boundary. The church contains an impressive Parish Chest and has many connections with the Bridgewater family.

3: A map of the whole Ashridge Estate has been provided to enable walkers to devise their own additional routes (page 117).

ASHRIDGE HOUSE

Edmund, son of Richard of Cornwall and grandson of King John, in the year 1283, founded the abbey at Asseruge in Hertfordshire, a little way from the manor of Bercamsted, in which he placed monks of the Order of Bonhommes, being the first house for that Order built in England. So records the annals. In fact, Edmund preferred living at Asseruge, for the comfort there was a considerable improvement on the conditions prevailing in Bercamsted Castle. The monastery lasted until 1539.

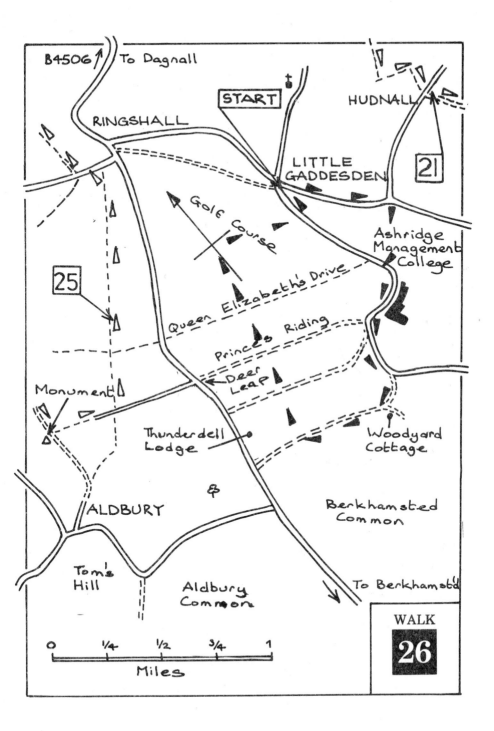

B4506 To Dagnall

RINGSHALL

START

HUDNALL

LITTLE GADDESDEN

21

Golf Course

Ashridge Management College

25

Queen Elizabeth's Drive

Princes Riding

Deer Leap

Monument

Thunderdell Lodge

Woodyard Cottage

Berkhamsted Common

ALDBURY

Tom's Hill

Aldbury Common

To Berkhamsted

0   ¼   ½   ¾   1

Miles

WALK
26

Until 1575 Ashridge House was a royal Tudor residence, then it became the home of the Egerton family, the most famous being Francis the third Duke of Bridgewater of canal-building repute. Through succeeding generations the monastic building fabric decayed, and when Ashridge went into the Brownlow branch of the family James Wyatt was commissioned for a new design in neo-Gothic – the house we see today – between the years 1808 and 1821.

An interesting feature near the house, but not well known, is an ice-house built in the shade of trees, seen as a bricklined passageway with internal doors. Inside is a 30' deep pit for use as a food-store, for no large house could be without one. Externally it looks like a grotto.

Ashridge Park started as a mediaeval deer park and in the course of time was divided, one part for red deer and the other for fallow which still roam freely. Landscaping of the park is a product of the works of Lancelot (Capability) Brown and Humphrey Repton, opening up Golden Valley, and the Prince's Riding avenue is a deer-leap, for the grounds were fully enclosed. Such spaces enabled deer to jump in but not escape, thus swelling herd numbers.

Most of the grounds entered the guardianship of the National Trust between 1926 and 1929 as the result of a nationwide appeal. The house was purchased by Mr Urban Broughton and he donated it to the Conservative Party so that the Bonar Law Memorial Trust might establish a College of Citizenship for training both party members and the general public. In the new constitution drawn up in 1954 the party affiliation ceased and the range of residential adult courses expanded, concentrating on aspects of management. It took the name of Ashridge Management College in 1959.

During the years 1940 to 1946 Ashridge House had served as an emergency wartime hospital having 12,000 beds in huts on the green open spaces in front of the house. The 1947-50 period saw the huts in use again for teacher training purposes then until their demolition they were used as the Ashridge Repository of the Public Record Office.

LITTLE GADDESDEN, ASHRIDGE MANAGEMENT COLLEGE, SOUTH AND EAST ESTATE LANDS

Little Gaddesden has a wealth of interesting vernacular architecture. On the corner of the church road stands John of Gaddesden's house, jettied and decorated with sun-burst pargetting. It is built with an end wing, and seen from the rear the accretions make for added visual interest. The tiled memorial, to those who fell in the Great War, is an arresting composition built into its front garden wall.

Going through the village watch for the many architectural details – the mullions, finials, cornices, fret-work, the squinched chimneys, window hoods, and much else. Especially see the fine gothic arched brickwork windows of the Red House and keep an eye open for the Brownlow coronets.

Another touching memorial, this time in the form of a cross surmounted on a plinth, is to Adelaide, the wife of the third Earl Brownlow, who was such a famous hostess to the great in the later Victorian era.

Cross over the road here entering the wooded slopes beside the field, then descending pass through the kissing-gate into Golden Valley. This recent acquisition for the National Trust is a grass vale bounded by hanging beech woods and leading into agricultural lands. Don't hurry, indeed the setting is so beautiful it is worth sitting down for a while, soaking up the 'feel' of the place. On the other side take the upward drive which joins the estate road.

Turn left towards the House, but before setting off glance back at the Adelaide Memorial in its commanding position above a grassy slope. Pass by the front of the house which is a feast of fretted castellations, window traceries and stained glass, pillasters, a steeple set with finials and a powerful central tower, all visually striking. The frontage is tied together by two terminal towers in a composition avoiding symmetry. Keep your eyes open for the long view towards the Monument as you pass the entrance, and in this vicinity will be a notice stating opening times for the gardens. Ashridge House's ice-house is situated in the woods near the southern extremity of the boundary fence.

Our way utilises the road for a short distance leaving the clear areas in front of the house, then on the second bend take the right hand Coldharbour drive which is a branch road pegged along its sides as a prevention from car parking. We pass a fir copse on the right as we bear right down the slope, meeting Woodyard cottage on the sharp left hand bend.

Now leave the drive by going forwards alongside an enclosed field in company with an avenue of mature beeches until reaching the end of the field. (The avenue is much used by strollers from cars parked in the clearings along the main roadside). Rise right through the trees on a little-used grassy path bordering this same field, which is the rear edge of Thunderdell Wood, and pass a small pond. Over the track ahead, taking the one rising on the gentle slope through young woodland and thus arriving on Prince's Riding.

This broad green swathe, popular with families, is the grand avenue, but look for a small stone-surfaced sidetrack a little to your left which passes by Old Park Lodge, a tower house with most unusual upward-curving soffits and a wall-mounted sundial above the entrance. Leave in the direction of the single-storeyed golf clubhouse on the far slope, first keeping right of the green in the foreground. Up the slope onto the club entrance road joining a tee junction. Turn right here past some very desirable residences. This access drive peters out into a simple track marked by white posts, eventually rejoining the golf fairways. Descending through an area of birches we make contact with the estate road.

Tring Reservoirs

Places included: MARSWORTH - BULBOURNE - LITTLE TRING - DRAYTON BEAUCHAMP - WILSTONE GREEN - TRINGFORD

Length of walk: 6 miles (can be shortened at will).

Start Grid Ref: Sheet 165 919141

Parking: Car-park at Startop Reservoir on the left immediately over the canal bridge coming from Ivinghoe. Also see Note 3.

Bus service: 61.

Public Houses: The White Lion, (Marsworth), The Angler's Retreat, (Marsworth), The Grand Junction Arms (Bulbourne).

Notes 1: This is a favourite haunt for hosts of anglers, the boating fraternity, walkers, natural history enthusiasts, artists and those just looking for somewhere pleasant to stroll. However, most stay near the canal or Startop Reservoir.

2: Just like the Ashridge Estates these reservoirs call one back time and time again, with the ever changing lighting effects from the open waters and the natural world responding to the seasonal changes. The area is very suitable for wintertime walking, but can be very bleak and cold.

3: If the car-park is full, as is often the case in summer months, find a spot not blocking farm gates in the Marsworth area, or start the walk along the route, say at Tringford.

4: The paths can be very muddy, so adequate footwear is recommended.

5: Binoculars are a must to make the most of the abundance of birdlife and the chance of heron sightings. Watch the edges of the waters for wildlife amongst the reeds.

TRING RESERVOIRS

Since time immemorial rivers have acted as highways and they still are the only means of communication in certain parts of the world. Even though improvements were made in many cases to make them navigable, as for instance

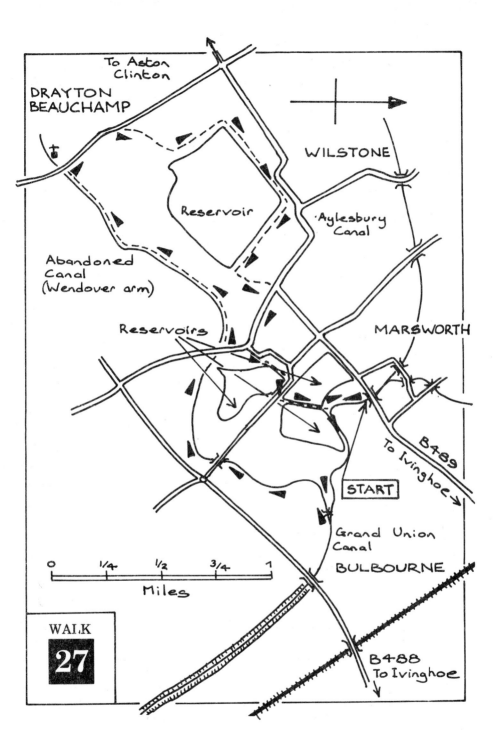

To Aston
Clinton

DRAYTON
BEAUCHAMP

WILSTONE

Reservoir

Aylesbury
Canal

Abandoned
Canal
(Wendover arm)

Reservoirs

MARSWORTH

B489

To Ivinghoe

START

Grand Union
Canal

BULBOURNE

0   1/4   1/2   3/4   1
Miles

B488
To Ivinghoe

WALK
27

123

the rivers Lea, Great Ouse and Stour (John Constable's river), there were problems with water supply and in passing water mills in the flash-locks. Sadly the rivers did not solve the problem of getting goods from A to B. Bear in mind that roads were an abomination because of mud, usable only by carts with very broad-rimmed wheels, if at all, for goods transport.

James Brindley's canal work in the 1760s for the 3rd Duke of Bridgewater – whereby he took a canal to a coalmine at Worsley crossing the R. Irewell by stone aqueduct into Manchester – eclipsed in the public's estimation all other canal projects and laid the foundations for Britain's canal system. The Grand Union Canal (formerly the Grand Junction) – a latecomer in canal history – opened at the turn of the nineteenth century. It was the work of William Jessop and made a direct connection between Brentford (on the R. Thames) and Birmingham. However this entailed traversing the Chilterns. The Tring Gap, already used by road (and later by rail), provided the best access at a height of 370 ft above sea level. Despite the absence of local streams, reservoirs of puddled clay – the same method employed in canal construction – were built; there were four in all between the years 1802 and 1817, also supplying water for the Aylesbury and Wendover arms. A steam-powered beam-engine (1803), housed at Tring Ford, pumped water into the reservoirs, until replaced by electric pumps in 1927.

Being at the summit, conservation of water as the working boats went through the locks was of prime importance, so sideponds were installed at Marsworth, saving half the water in the lock. The Tring Reservoirs are now a designated Nature Reserve of interest both for their water-loving flora and mammals and even more especially for ornithology. Herons, coots, moorhens, grebes and many other species use the waters as a stopover.

WALK 27

MARSWORTH, BULBOURNE, LITTLE TRING, DRAYTON BEAUCHAMP, WILSTONE GREEN, TRINGFORD

Leave the car park by its far end, crossing a small brook, and go out onto the canal towpath. Immediately the tree-fringed expanses of water make an impact, with the St. Leonard's wooded Chiltern Hills forming a backdrop for the scene.

The canalside path passes the return route from between two neighbouring waters, with reeds and rushes at their edges and skirted with trees. Several bends in the canal are encountered before reaching Marsworth locks alongside the trim lockkeeper's house, with the now defunct sideponds once used for conserving water in these summit stretches of the canal. Children are fascinated by watching the locking of boats.

We stay with the canal until the Wendover Arm is met beside the canal house, using the footbridge for the crossing. As an added experience you can walk up to Bulbourne and see the canalside workshops of Inland Waterways, having a 19th century range of buildings for boat and lockgate work. Then gaze in awe at the nearly two mile long deep cutting ahead beyond the bridge crossing the Chilterns summit – a laborious digging task by pick, shovel and wheel-barrow. (The spoil is on the north bank). Not far away is the famed Tring railway cutting mentioned in several railway histories, especially "The Railway Navvies" by Terry Coleman.

Retracing our footsteps we follow the Wendover canal branch – a store for disused working boats; this stretch traverses open fields offering a more expansive feel looking out northwards across the Vale of Aylesbury. Now through a patch of trees onto the road, turning left past Tring flour mills, then right at the Tring Wharf roundabout, passing a small housing estate. After 500 yards or so right again following the old Tring canal arm. (All towns wanted their own canal connections by the turn of the 19th century if it was at all possible, for coal, chinaware, slates and all commodities lending themselves to bulk water-borne transportation.)

Having rejoined the Wendover Arm continue until the Little Tring pumping station is reached and the finish of the 'cut' containing water. Now through the bushes, arriving on the road and turning right, being very careful as cars travel fast past the cottages on the bend. A clearly marked way leaves the road on your left, uniting us with the dry bed of the canal. Extensive scrub clearance in recent years has revealed the canal cross-section and it is not difficult to visualise the draught of the working boats and just how much clearance they had.

On the good path the going is easy, and so enjoy the views out over Wilstone reservoir and the sight of Marsworth church on a high position in the north. Ivinghoe Beacon dominates the horizon behind you.

We arrive at the bridge of Drayton Beauchamp close by an absolute gem of a country church with its tree lined churchyard, delightful in springtime particularly, hard by the wooded gorge of the canal course. Down the road for about half a mile watching for the stile on your right hand side just past Upper Farm, which leads to a path that diagonally crosses the meadows towards a treebelt.

Crossing the next stile bear left to find that this is a wooded stretch beside the water. Right at the end of this 'corridor' we find ourselves now on the high banks of Wilstone reservoir – continue clockwise on the next two sides. Into the small copse in the far corner then left along the track. This right of way meets the road tee-junction beside the rural Tringford cemetary. Right uphill past the "road travellers' caravans" and over the brow, watching out next for the concealed slip-road left at the bend.

Further Walking Areas

Bedfordshire County Council Walks.

1. The Greensand Ridge Walk (see below)

2. Circular walks based on the Greensand Ridge Walk

   a. Woburn Abbey/Aspley Guise   11 miles
   b. Ampthill/Millbrook   6 miles
   c. Old Warden   7 miles

3. Three Circular Walks from Dunstable Downs. These are Walks compiled in conjunction with Dunstable Town Council varying from 2½ to 4½ miles and taking in Totternhoe and the outskirts of Dunstable beside the golf course.

Edlesborough. No walks are included in this book taking in Eaton Bray/ Edlesborough district, as it is riddled with minor roads and few footpaths. Edlesborough to Ivinghoe, commencing on the broad track beside the church pass by Ivinghoe Aston, then alongside Crabtree Cottage and down by the Ivinghoe golf course. The walk provides a fine panorama of the Downs and Whipsnade Chalk Lion. The return can be by footpaths from Ivinghoe, via Ford End (watermill) Ivinghoe Aston, the Butler's Farm and the A4146.

Grand Union Canal. The towpath can be walked anywhere from Berkhamsted, Tring, Marsworth (reservoirs see Walk 27), Slapton, Leighton Buzzard, Stoke Hammond and Bletchley.

The Greens. (Ref Walk 14). Mangrove Green, Cockernhoe Green, Tea Green, Chiltern Green, Peter's Green, Breachwood Green, Wanden and Diamond Ends, provide a network of country roads and some footpaths east of Luton Airport.

The Greensand Ridge Walk. Opened in 1987 and almost entirely in Bedfordshire. This 40 mile Walk leaves Leighton Buzzard by the canal through Woburn Park, Ampthill, Clophill, Hayes, Northill, and Sandy, finishing in Gamlingay (Cambs). Full waymarking is employed and a map of the definitive route can be obtained from Beds C.C. Leisure Service Dept. (Muntjac deer is the symbol).

Harpenden. (Ref Walk 17). Harpenden makes a good staging place for walks in the outskirts of St Albans, Brocket Hall Park, Wheathampstead and Ayot St Lawrence and Ayot St Peter.

The Ridgeway. (Ref Walk 25). This long distance path terminates on Ivinghoe Beacon and is waymarked in its entirety. The stretches through Wendover, Coombe Hill, Whiteleaf Hill down to Chinnor and beyond make excellent walks. (Acorn is the symbol).

Stockgrove Park. Heath and Reach, Leighton Buzzard is a country park under the management of Bedfordshire C.C., and being on the Greensand acid soil has encouraged coniferous woodland around an artificial lake. There are plenty of paths within the grounds and it is a good location for natural history lovers. Guidebook available. Entrance on the Gt Brickhill road out of Heath and Reach. (No charge).

Tiddenfoot Lake. On the Ivinghoe road out of Leighton Buzzard (Sheet 165 915238) B488, is an exhausted sandpit that has had its banks planted with trees plus natural colonisation and makes a pleasant area for a short walk or using its jogging course. The canal is alongside together with other quarry workings. The Tiddenfoot Leisure Centre is not far away.

The Waldens. (Ref Walk 14). The area King's and St. Pauls Walden with Preston, Whitwell and Bendish makes excellent rambling country, included frequently on several rambling clubs' programmes.

Whipsnade Commons. (Ref Walk 24). The commons can be roamed with the Tree Cathedral (National Trust) making an interesting excursion, planted as a memorial for the friends of Edmund Blyth, killed in the First World War.

The commons can be a start for visitors' own walks, starting from the new part at the crossroads through the cleared way and through the scrub out to Kensworth or down the Markyate road.

Woburn. Woburn Abbey Deer and Safari Park has footpaths, but use maps for correct courses, for it is a splendid way of seeing the park which is traversed by the Greensand Ridge Walk – Woburn/Bow Brickhill Woods. From Little Brickhill in the south to Aspley Heath in the north these heaths and woods on the sandy soils with the many paths and bridleways make an ideal ground for diverse walks.

Selected Places of Interest

Ashridge House gardens
Ayot St. Lawrence (Shaw's Corner and village churches)
Berkhamsted Castle
Chiltern Open Air Museum, Chalfont St. Peter
Hatfield House
Houghton House, Ampthill
Ivinghoe Water Mill
Knebworth House
Leighton Buzzard Light Railway
Luton Airport (spectators' enclosure)
Luton Hoo Collection
Luton Museum and Art Gallery
Piccott's End Mediaeval Wallpaintings and Museum, Hemel Hempstead
Pitstone Farm Museum
Pitstone Windmill
St. Albans City Museum
St. Albans Verulam Museum (Roman displays)
Stockwood Park Museum, Luton (craft displays)
Tring Natural History Museum
Whipsnade Zoo
Woburn Abbey House; Deer and Safari Park
Woodside Wild Fowl, near Caddington

Further reading

Beds C.C. County Planning Dept.	Brickmaking – a history and gazeteer	Beds C.C.
Beds C.C. County Planning Dept.	Glossary of Terms – historic landscape and archaeology	Beds C.C.
Bedfordshire Natural History Society	Bedfordshire Wildlife	Castlemead
Bellamy, David	"You can't see the wood. . . " (Leaflet)	BBC tv/English Tourist Board
Benson, Nigel	Dunstable in Detail	Book Castle
Burden, Vera	Discovering the Ridgeway	Shire Publications
Brunskill, R.W	Vernacular Architecture	Faber
Dyer, James and Dony, John	The Story of Luton	White Crescent Press
Evans, Vivienne	The Book of Dunstable and Houghton Regis	Barracuda Books
Evans, Vivienne	History All Around	Book Castle
Godber, Joyce	History of Bedfordshire	Beds C.C.
Hawes, Hugh	Bedfordshire Windmills	County Planning Dept Beds C.C.
Hodgkins, A.G.	Discovering Antique Maps	Shire Publications
Hoskins, W.G.	Making of the English Countryside	Penguin Books
Lovering, Pat	Old Houghton	Book Castle
Lovering, Pat	Royal Houghton	Book Castle
Mackay, Anthony	Journeys into Bedfordshire	Book Castle
Meadows, Eric	Pictorial Guide to Bedfordshire	White Crescent Press
Peters, J.E.C.	Discovering Traditional Farm Buildings	Shire Publications
Ramblers' Association	Hedgerows – Lifelines of our Countryside (Leaflet)	Ramblers' Association

P.S. Two magazines also publish informative and invaluable articles – 'Bedfordshire Magazine' (quarterly) and 'Northamptonshire and Bedfordshire Life' (monthly).

Organisations

Walking

South Beds Group of the Ramblers' Association
Luton Ramblers
Youth Hostel Association
(ask at the local libraries for the names of Secretaries)

Countryside

Leisure Services Dept., Beds C.C. — Open spaces and amenities responsibilities.

County Ranger Service, Beds C.C. — Countryside caretakers, management schemes and public information, etc.

The National Trust, Thames and Chilterns Region, Hughenden Manor, High Wycombe.

English Tourist Board, Thames and Chilterns Area, The Mount House, Witney, Oxfordshire.

Pitstone Local History Society, Pitstone Green Farm, Pitstone, Bucks — Ivinghoe Watermill, Pitstone Farm Museum and Pitstone Windmill information.

Rambling Holidays

Countrywide Holidays Association (C.H.A.), Birch Heys, Cromwell Range, Manchester M14 6HU

Holiday Fellowship, (H.F.), 142/144 Great North Way, London NW4 1EG

Ramblers' Holidays Ltd., PO Box 43, Welwyn Garden City, Herts.

Bus Services

The bus route information given below has been furnished from the Bedfordshire County Council Bus Guide and was correct at the time of going to press. Routes however are reviewed, changed or terminated and enquiry is advisable before your excursion.

Bus route nos. for the walks.

		Operator
22	Luton – Leagrave – Sundon	L&D
24	Luton – Leagrave – Toddington – Ampthill	L&D
34	Dunstable – Houghton Regis – Leagrave	BUFF
38	Luton Airport – Houghton Regis – Dunstable	L&D
39	Stopsley – Houghton Regis – Dunstable	L&D
43	Luton – Dunstable – Kensworth – Studham – Hemel Hempstead	BUFF
61	Luton – Dunstable – Edlesborough – Aylesbury	L&D
63	Bedford – Ampthill – Toddington – Dunstable	BUFF
65	Bedford – Wilstead – Ampthill – Toddington – Dunstable	BUFF
69	Luton – Dunstable – Hockliffe – Leighton Buzzard	L&D
70	Luton – Dunstable – Stanbridge – Leighton Buzzard	L&D
71	Totternhoe – Edlesborough – Leighton Buzzard	L&D
72	Edlesborough – Dagnall – Dunstable	L&D
75	Flitwick – Ampthill – Luton	BUFF
76	Luton – Barton	L&D
78	Luton – Barton – Shefford – Henlow Camp	L&D
79	Luton – Barton – Shefford – Henlow Camp	L&D
92	Luton – Hitchin – Baldock	L&D
93	Luton – Hitchin – Baldock	L&D
94	Luton – Hitchin – Baldock	L&D
95	Luton – Hitchin – Baldock	L&D
96	Luton – Hitchin – Stotfold	L&D
97	Luton – Hitchin – Stotfold	L&D
98	Luton – Hitchin – Stotfold	L&D
99	Luton – Hitchin – Baldock	L&D
139	Woburn Sands – Hockliffe – Leighton Buzzard	VILLBUS
142	Bedford – Ampthill – Dunstable	UC
230	Luton – Caddington	HOP
231	Luton – Caddington – Dunstable	HOP
232	Luton – Caddington – Dunstable	HOP
245	Luton – Dunstable – Studham	HOP

268	Luton – Dunstable – Leighton Buzzard	HOP
343	Dunstable – Markyate – St. Albans	BUFF
545	Luton – Dunstable – Hockliffe – Milton Keynes	L&D
652	Dunstable – Houghton Regis – London	L&D
755	Dunstable – Markyate – London	L&D

Bus Operators

BUFF	Buffalo Travel, Flitwick.
HOP	Hoppanstopper, Luton and District Transport.
L&D	Luton and District Transport including:
	Aylesbury Bus
	Dunstable Bus
	Hoppanstopper
	Luton Bus
VILLBUS	R. F. Litchfield, 'Village Bus', Woburn.
UC	United Counties Omnibus Co. Ltd., Bedford.

Index

Notes

Contents of the Companion Volume to this Book
LOCAL WALKS BOOK 2
NORTH AND MID-BEDFORDSHIRE

Index Maps for the Companion Volume to this Book
LOCAL WALKS BOOK 2
NORTH AND MID-BEDFORDSHIRE

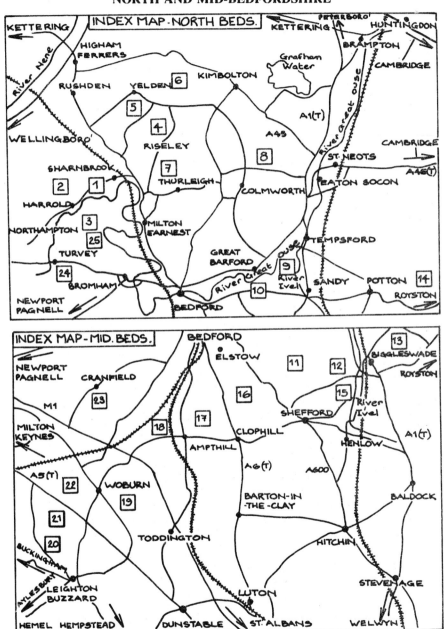

Books Published by
THE BOOK CASTLE

NORTH CHILTERNS CAMERA, 1863–1954; FROM THE THURSTON COLLECTION IN LUTON MUSEUM: Edited by Stephen Bunker
Rural landscapes, town views, studio pictures and unique royal portraits by the area's leading early photographer.

JOURNEYS INTO BEDFORDSHIRE: Anthony Mackay
Foreword by The Marquess of Tavistock
A lavish book of over 150 evocative ink drawings.

FOLK: CHARACTERS and EVENTS in the HISTORY OF BEDFORDSHIRE and NORTHAMPTONSHIRE: Vivienne Evans
Arranged by village/town, an anthology of stories about the counties' most intriguing historical figures.

ECHOES: TALES and LEGENDS of BEDFORDSHIRE and HERTFORDSHIRE: Vic Lea
Thirty, compulsively retold historical incidents.

TERESA of WATLING STREET: Arnold Bennett
Introduced by Simon Houfe
The only detective story by one of the twentieth century's most famous novelists. Written and set in Bedfordshire.

A LASTING IMPRESSION: Michael Dundrow
An East End boy's war-time experiences as an evacuee on a Chiltern farm at Totternhoe.

JOHN BUNYAN: HIS LIFE and TIMES: Vivienne Evans
Foreword by the Bishop of Bedford
Bedfordshire's most famous son set in his seventeenth century context.

LOCAL WALKS: SOUTH BEDFORDSHIRE and NORTH CHILTERNS: Vaughan Basham
Twenty-seven thematic circular walks.

LOCAL WALKS: NORTH and MID-BEDFORDSHIRE: Vaughan Basham
A further twenty-five original thematic circular walks.

DUNSTABLE DECADE: THE EIGHTIES – A collection of photographs: Pat Lovering
A souvenir book of nearly 300 pictures of people and events in the 1980s.

DUNSTABLE IN DETAIL: Nigel Benson
A hundred of the town's buildings and features, past and present, plus town-trail map.

OLD DUNSTABLE: Bill Twaddle
A new edition of this collection of early photographs.

BOURNE and BRED: A DUNSTABLE BOYHOOD BETWEEN THE WARS: Colin Bourne
Portrait of home and town, church and school, characters and countryside.

ROYAL HOUGHTON: Pat Lovering
Illustrated history of Houghton Regis from earliest times to the present day.

OLD HOUGHTON, INCLUDING UPPER HOUGHTON, NOW PART OF DUNSTABLE: Pat Lovering
Over 170 photographs of Houghton Regis during the last 100 years.

Further titles are in preparation.
All the above are available via any bookshop,
or from the publisher and bookseller
THE BOOK CASTLE
12 Church Street, Dunstable, Bedfordshire LU5 4RU. Tel (0582) 605670